JEAN ANOUILH

JEAN ANOUILH

JEAN ANOUILH

POET OF PIERROT AND PANTALOON

by

EDWARD OWEN MARSH

NEW YORK / RUSSELL & RUSSELL

FOR NUSHKA

FIRST PUBLISHED IN 1953
BY W. H. ALLEN & COMPANY, LTD., LONDON
REISSUED, 1968, BY RUSSELL & RUSSELL
A DIVISION OF ATHENEUM HOUSE, INC.
BY ARRANGEMENT WITH W. H. ALLEN & COMPANY, LTD.
L. C. CATALOG CARD NO: 68-25041
PRINTED IN THE UNITED STATES OF AMERICA

Contents

Contents

Illustrations

"Amour, triste amour, tu es content? Cher cœur, cher corps, chère romance. Est-ce qu'on n'a pas de métiers à faire, des livres à lire, des maisons à bâtir? Est-ce que ce n'est pas bon, aussi, le soleil sur la peau, le vin frais dans le verre, l'eau du ruisseau, l'ombre à midi, le feu l'hiver, la neige et la pluie même, et le vent, et les arbres, et les nuages, et les bêtes, toutes les bêtes innocentes, et les enfants avant qu'ils ne deviennent trop laids? Triste amour, dis, est-ce que tout aussi n'est pas bon?"

Roméo et Jeannette

Author's Foreword

Answering a request for biographical details Jean Anouilh wrote to Hubert Gignoux in 1945:

"I have no biography, and I am very glad of it. I was born in Bordeaux on the 23rd of June, 1910. I came to Paris when I was young and attended the Colbert Primary School and later Chaptal College. A year and a half at the Law Faculty in Paris, then two years in an advertising firm, where I learned to be ingenious and exact, lessons that for me took the place of studies in literature. After my play *L'Hermine* was produced I decided to live only by writing for the theatre, and a little for films. It was folly, but I did right to make that decision. I have managed never to touch journalism, and in films all I have on my conscience are one or two cheap farces and a few unsigned and now forgotten romantic melodramas. The rest is my life, and for as long as it pleases Heaven for it to be my private business, I shall keep the details to myself."

So this book is not a biography of Jean Anouilh. It gives the biographical essentials but that is all. My concern has been to present Jean Anouilh's twenty years of dramatic writing in a way that will help English playgoers and readers to a wider acquaintance with the most gifted dramatist of our generation.

At the outset let me say that I have not aimed at assessing Anouilh's "philosophic" ideas, and I have not argued particularly for or against them. I hope to have explained them clearly, but however valid his pessimism may be philosophically his dramatic skill will be undisputed. Who bothers about the validity of the greater part of Strindberg's views? I leave the reader to make up his own mind whether or not Jean Anouilh's vision of the human condition adds anything to his own.

The middle part of the book is envisaged as a reference section covering all the plays to date. In that section I have done little more than bring out the particular qualities of each play, as I preferred to reserve general comments for the final chapter. Some plays are dealt with more fully as they are clearly of greater importance in Anouilh's development.

Jean Anouilh is in the prime of life, a comparatively young man, and we can only hope that he is in no more than mid-career. This is not the time for a final judgment on his work, but it is the time for making it generally known to the thinking public. Posterity will settle his permanent reputation without our help and scholars will be busy a hundred years hence proving that whatever we, his contemporaries, said about Anouilh, we were wrong.

This is the book of an enthusiast and it is written simply for readers and theatre-goers who want more of Jean Anouilh than the London stage can or will provide.

I thought it best not to develop close comparisons with other dramatists or to dig into details of style, since in both cases this would have led to constant reference to plays and playwrights of modern France known only to a few English readers. I have therefore remained throughout on general ground. More concentrated criticism is for the academic works of the future and is purposely excluded from this book.

I hope that the illustrations will bring back to some readers, as they do to me, memories of many exquisite moments we owe to Jean Anouilh in the theatres of both London and Paris.

No writer on Anouilh can fail to acknowledge his debt to the most penetrating study of his drama so far published: Hubert Gignoux's *Jean Anouilh* (Editions du Temps Présent, 1946), a model of moral analysis.

I would like to express my thanks to: Methuen and Co., Ltd, for permission to quote from their English published translations of *Ardèle, Colombe, Antigone, Eurydice, Ring Round the Moon*; Mr Carl Wildman for the use of his version of *Léocadia*; André Barsacq, Director of the Atelier Theatre, for pictures of himself and Jean Anouilh, and of the French productions of *Antigone, Le Bal des Voleurs,*

Le Rendez-vous de Senlis, Colombe, L'Invitation au Château; M. Jean Flory, of the Atelier Theatre, for many years of generous help in matters connected with the French theatre as a whole and this work on Jean Anouilh in particular; M. Claude Sainval, Director of La Comédie des Champs-Elysées, for pictures of his fine productions of *Ardèle* and *La Valse des Toréadors*; and M. Jean-Louis Barrault for pictures of his production of *La Répétition* at the Marigny Theatre. Last but not least I would like to thank my publishers for their patience and understanding.

London, July, 1952   EDWARD OWEN MARSH

1

Beginnings

"Tout le monde ne peut pas être orphelin."
(JULES RENARD, *Poil de Carotte*)

A little more than fifty years ago an outraged leader in the London *Daily Telegraph* called Ibsen's *Ghosts* "an open drain, a loathsome sore unbandaged, a dirty act done publicly, a lazar-house with all its windows open". A torrent of realism has flowed across the English footlights since then and we pride ourselves now on being more broadminded. We have given the morality of the Victorians close scrutiny and vowed never to be such hypocrites again, while the offending Ibsen has become a classic. Now that we have digested Shaw, Lawrence and Huxley we are inclined to feel full emancipation is achieved.

But broadmindedness is not enough – it is a quality of mind only. Its value is relative – to narrowmindedness – and our temporary preoccupation with it prevented us from seeing that not only our ideas but also our feelings needed emancipation. Dressed in our new broadmindedness we felt like the Emperor in his New Clothes, very smart and sensible, never to be taken in again. But like him we went on seeing what we imagined instead of having a good stare at what was there. For it is one thing to liberate the mind from its intellectual bonds and quite another to feel simply and say freely all that is in one's heart – we lacked the direct expression of emotion. Though the taboos were swept away much of the rigidity was barely dusted and the Englishman is still verbally stiff with his emotions.

A return to fuller expression in the theatre – and speech is the flesh and blood of dramatic art – is to be seen in our younger playwrights Christopher Fry, Peter Ustinov, Dennis Cannan, John Whiting and others, but there is a coldness about their works that confines them to intellectual drama. They are infusing new warmth into the language but still largely outside the field of individual emotion. Their success nevertheless is significant of a deep desire for change. In the last decade or two a feeling has been growing that our national reticence is not a virtue in itself; British phlegm has had its day. The full life is not easy to live in silence and in fear of words, our emotions are falsified by the very fact of their inadequate expression. The urgency of war brought us out of ourselves, the restrictions of post-war economy drove us back. More contacts with foreigners got us over some of our embarrassment at more demonstrative ways of feeling, but if we want to let ourselves go we come up against the barrier of a language that has been pauperised by hypocrisy. Victorian pretence has gone from our thoughts but the language has not recovered – when our thoughts struggle to fly we find their wings are clipped, for our emotional vocabulary is a sham.

Nowhere is this fact more apparent than in the theatre, where we find the directness of foreign plays, especially from France, takes our breath away. The English dramatist still dare not be honest with his feelings, and the good French dramatist wins easily every time in his handling of emotion. Perhaps we are at the moment of transition – the French invasion looks capable of sweeping the remnants of our emotional self-consciousness before it and bringing public, censor and, not least important, theatre-managers face to face with new needs. There has been a "silent revolution" in culture as well as in politics since the end of the 'thirties. It is significant to see some critics assert that English audiences take from French authors what they would never take from our own. But what contemporary English dramatist has offered anything comparable with what Anouilh offers – in spite of the pessimism that was found to be so indigestible by one famous critic? The audience's enthusiasm for something new should be an encouraging fact, not excuse for lamentation – it broadens the field for the future. The new conditions will produce new dramatists.

Many of these reflections were prompted by seeing a Birmingham audience thoroughly exhilarated by Jean Anouilh's outspoken play *Ardèle*. This solidly English audience loved the play, and the critics (including one or two from London) were full of praise. After the London opening, however, the critics of the national press, with only one or two dissentients, damned the play roundly, and several newspapers printed notices that reminded us of the indignant leader of the 'nineties about Ibsen's *Ghosts*.

Here are some of the more violent opinions expressed:

". . . the fashionable M. Anouilh here gives us as distasteful and offensive a play as ever saw a stage."

". . . with all the aid of Anouilh's masterly but evilly misdirected sense of theatre, a dirty hand is smeared across the picture and sentiment is turned to gruesome obscenity."

". . . it is a slimy, decadent, demoralised and singularly repulsive exhibit. As a spectacle it is of a piece with the main-street antics of the less fastidious canines. . . ."

". . . the ugliest and most nauseating play I have ever seen . . . furtive, slinking, bedroom keyhole humour."

". . . an evening which is one long wallow of unedifying lechery has left me still completely in

the dark as to its justification on grounds of art,
philosophy, dramatic skill or entertainment."

In the London production some of the major
parts were sadly miscast and the playing was so far
off the spirit of the play that even Anouilh's sparkling dialogue came over as dull. I have rarely been
so stimulated in the theatre in my life as I was at the
Paris production of this play; the London production, with much more distinguished actors, I found
tedious. The critics made the mistake of attacking
the play when in fact much of Anouilh's gifted
theatricality had been ironed out of it. The play
had simply not been understood even in theatrical
terms, for as one critic noted at the time, even
specific stage instructions from Anouilh in the
French had been deliberately ignored (for details
see section on *Ardèle* in Chapter 2). The London
audience was being shown something very different
from the play Jean Anouilh wrote, although the
text had been very faithfully and intelligently translated. All the life had been removed, it was con-
sistently inadequate, misfiring like a damp squib,
as undramatic as if at Mrs Higgins' tea-party Eliza
Doolittle had spoken perfect English.

But it is a sure sign of power and originality when
an artist's work arouses the extremes of emotion.
The plays of Jean Anouilh are either judged to be
important works of art containing the philosophic
resonances that are the signs of genius, or they are

dismissed as trivial melodramas in a novel tone. No one would deny the melodrama or the triviality to be found in his work, but there is gravity and pure tragedy too. His peculiar contribution to the theatre is this very mixture of opposites – the tragic and the ludicrous, the realistic and the romantic, the serious and the trivial go hand in hand throughout his plays. He has discovered new dramatic tones through the interplay of contrasting moods. The plays, the majority labelled *Pièces Roses* and *Pièces Noires* (reminding us of Shaw's *Plays Pleasant* and *Plays Unpleasant*), are all tragi-comedies. It is the emphasis that makes them *rose* or *noir*.

Yet nothing is blurred. Anouilh has the unerring choice of words and image, the poetry of the commonplace that marks the born dramatist. Not a word is wasted, and there is an inevitability in the dialogue and characters that afterwards freezes the momentary theatrical effects into permanence. The most trivial things in his airiest plays seem strangely significant, for as a craftsman he has no equal among his contemporaries. However much the plays seem to follow a formula and represent a philosophy, they are not *pièces à thèse* – Anouilh is primarily a dramatist, not a philosopher.

It is his ideas that have made him the most striking, and his remarkable sense of theatre that has made him the most powerful dramatist of recent years. This does not mean that his ideas are particularly profound or that they are even sympathetic to the vast majority of people – less to English than to French minds, without doubt – but they are arresting, often deeply disturbing, and always impressively sincere.

Jean Anouilh is an elusive person and nowhere has he committed himself to anything resembling a full biographical statement. He has provided no material for the gossip columnists other than news of his frequent voyages – almost the only ''story'' is of his using a telescope during the Occupation, on his fifth-floor balcony in Montmartre, to spy out the new deliveries of vegetables at the local shops. Very few people meet him except when his plays are produced (for he is passionately interested in the proper production of his work), and even on those occasions he seldom speaks to the Press.

Jean Anouilh was born in Bordeaux on June 23rd, 1910. His father was a tailor, his mother a violinist. As a boy of eight he saw numerous operettas at the Casino at Arcachon where his mother played in the orchestra – but he always had to leave at the interval to go to bed. Thus he knew the whole range of operettas without ever seeing how one ended.

''When I was ten,'' Anouilh said in an interview for *Les Nouvelles Littéraires* in 1937, ''I was already writing plays, and they were in verse, imitations of Edmond Rostand. I wrote Cyrano all over again. But I only managed short plays – one-acters, or plays where three acts would play for much less than an hour. I was sixteen before I wrote a play that was as long as a real play. I found that play and re-read it recently – it was not too bad . . . . The title was "The Woman on the Mantelpiece" – it is the story of a man who has too much respect for a woman and stands her on the mantelpiece . . . . if you see what I mean ?"

He moved to Paris at a very early age and after leaving school studied law for a year and a half at the University, but was obliged to go out into the world and earn his living. He took a job in an advertising firm, earning his keep by singing the praises of Peugeot cars and Valisère underwear. Other writers employed by the firm were also literary men and with them Jean Anouilh made his first attempts at creative writing – they were responsible for some of the first publicity films in Europe. They all at times acted in their films as well as wrote them, though at no time with this firm did Anouilh earn more than three thousand francs a month. Later he supplemented this by selling comic gags for films at a hundred francs a time. It was at this period that he met Monelle Valentin, the young actress who was soon to become his wife and who was the inspiration for many of the young girl parts in the plays to come.

The advertising work was not lucrative but at least he was in congenial company. With one of his colleagues, Jean Aurenche, he wrote a farcical one-acter called *Humulus le Muet*, the story of a young man to whom nature had denied the power of saying more than one word per day. The young Humulus builds up a stock of these single words for weeks and at last blurts them all out in romantic admiration to a girl he has mutely loved since he first met her. This ten-minute extravaganza is today a popular play in amateur societies throughout France.

A few months after *Humulus*, in 1929, Anouilh wrote his own first long play, *Mandarine*. This was not produced until three years later, in 1933, at the Athénée, and has been called an adolescent mistake. Like so many of his later plays this first effort was about the hypocrisy men are prepared to countenance for the sake of money. An innocent young girl, with a missionary passion for the redemption of sinners, wastes her pure love on trying to save a smooth gigolo whom his unsavoury friends have nicknamed "Mandarine". (This title name was a private joke on Anouilh's friend Aurenche – "orange".) The play did not hang together and though the critics saw in it signs of skill in handling characters and dialogue they were not very impressed. Anouilh has not published the play among his works.

In 1931 Georges Neveux (author of *Plainte contre Inconnu* and *Le Voyage de Thésée*, and of brilliant French translations of *Othello* and *A Midsummer Night's Dream*) retired from his post as secretary to Louis Jouvet's company, and the twenty-year-old Jean Anouilh took his place. This brought the ambitious dramatist right into the world of the theatre, but Jouvet showed little interest in him. He even nicknamed him "Anouilh le Miteux" and told him, not without good cause at the time, "There'll always be a bowl of soup for you here if you need it!" When shortly afterwards the penniless Anouilh was married to Monelle Valentin and wanted to start a home, Jouvet lent him the imitation furniture (all false doors and drawers) from Giraudoux's *Siegfried*, which had just ended its run at the theatre. Naturally enough he asked for it back when he revived the play.

It was Pierre Fresnay who gave Anouilh his first real chance. His warm recommendation persuaded Paulette Pax to produce the first serious play, *L'Hermine*, at her theatre, L'Œuvre, when Anouilh was only twenty-two years of age. The play (of which more in the next chapter of this book) ran for a modest thirty-seven performances. For the following three years Anouilh lived in comparative poverty and disappointment – the plays he wrote, later to be great successes (*Le Bal des Voleurs*, *La Sauvage*), were everywhere rejected by theatre managers. Towards the end of this period a daughter, Catherine, was born and passed her first few months in a suitcase for a cradle.

Suddenly in 1935 came the production of *Y Avait Un Prisonnier* at the Théâtre des Ambassadeurs, and it marks the turning of the tide. The first night was a brilliant success, but in spite of that, and the notices, the play failed to draw the public. It was a freak success that made people talk but it was not a very good play, and Anouilh has consigned it to oblivion with *Mandarine*. A Hollywood company immediately paid heavily for the film rights, however, and the Anouilh fortunes were at once out of the mire. The family had its first car, Catherine had a cot, and Jean Anouilh realised his dearest dream – he bought a home of his own.

From this time on Anouilh found film-scripts to write and kept the family in comparative comfort. (His work on scenarios is outside the scope of this book but some well-known films have come from his pen: *Caroline Chérie*, *Cavalcade d'Amour*, *Monsieur Vincent*, *Anna Karénine* and *Deux Sous de Violettes* – this last being based on a novel by Monelle Valentin. I have also put aside as outside my aim Anouilh's small contribution to ballet – the result of a ski accident at Marzine in 1948, where he met Roland Petit and wrote at his invitation what became the ballet *Les Demoiselles de la Nuit*.) Not until nearly three years later, in 1937, did he have his first financial success in the theatre, when perhaps the poorest theatre-director in Paris, Georges Pitoëff, produced what is generally considered to be one of Anouilh's finest plays, *Le Voyageur Sans Bagages*. This production put the seal on his reputation and marked him as one of the most interesting younger dramatists. In the next few years an Anouilh play was presented nearly every season at the Théâtre de l'Atelier : *Le Rendez-vous de Senlis* before the war ; early in the war *Léocadia* and *Eurydice*, with revivals of *Le Bal des Voleurs* and *Le Voyageur Sans Bagages*; towards the end of the war *Antigone*; soon after the Liberation *Roméo et Jeannette* and *L'Invitation au Château*.

Thus it was only after he had become very well established in France that Anouilh was noticed by the rest of the world. The war had boxed writers up within their national frontiers ; immediately there was freer movement Anouilh began to be translated, and was presented in Milan, Stockholm, Vienna, New York, and at last London. Anouilh himself lives most untheatrically : he shuns publicity and dodges the gossip-writers, fully deserving his reputation as an unsociable recluse. In person Anouilh is a very modest man in his early forties who wears simple clothes and gold-rimmed spectacles. As can be seen from the frontispiece and the photographs facing page 112, his short black hair and vigorous eyes make him look rather younger than his age, but he has a nervous concentration that seems to counter his striking youthfulness. His conversation is unusually lucid and colourful, for he drops unhesitatingly on the exact word he requires – there is an almost legal precision in his terms and a vivid artistic compactness in image. He talks as he writes.

Immediately after the Liberation of France *Les Lettres Françaises*, a Communist-controlled newspaper, took exception to many of Creon's speeches in *Antigone*, where it is argued that power must of necessity involve compromise but that somebody always has to accept responsibility. Anouilh was accused of vindicating the Vichy régime through the character of Creon, but the charge was soon seen by everyone to be preposterous and was dropped.

The simple fact is that there is very little in *Antigone* that cannot be found in all Anouilh's work long before the war. Corruption is Anouilh's constant theme. Not the corruption of power alone, but the way society corrupts any individual. A child's nature is pure, but as a child cannot bloom unseen in the desert and must grow up a member of a community, its purity is bound thereby to be spoiled. Pride, selfishness, hatred, violence, mistrust, revenge – all these monsters of poisoned feeling rise from our basic purity when it is, as it must be, thwarted and overridden. In all his contacts with other humans the individual suffers as he changes – he is never left to develop freely. The child is dependent on his parent's love, but imperceptibly that love deteriorates into an oppressive habit that destroys its charge. The grown man may forget he ever did struggle to grow into anything different, and may live the rest of his life faithful to the picture of himself that his friends and relations have constructed. But some see the lie, hate this false self which has been imposed on them, long to be free and are filled with shame.

Anouilh is a pessimist because he has a burning desire for a personal perfection that is unattainable in this world. This nostalgia for individual purity marks even his cruellest scenes with poetry and speaks to our innermost selves. His is no ordinary youthful idealism, for youth is optimistic. On the contrary he speaks with experience and full consciousness. We have all known those moments of disgust and despair when visions have flashed upon us of pure love, and sublime feelings, which will never come again. Mostly we accept this fall from grace as general and inevitable, and we know there are no exceptions – among the living at least. This is the mood of Anouilh's *Pièces Roses*. But at times death appears preferable to going on living burdened forever with such an overwhelming sense of loss and inadequacy – this is the mood of his *Pièces Noires*. Both, however, spring from the same intense feeling of shame and longing. Anouilh has fixed these haunting moments in works of art, all of which tell the story of mankind's doomed purity in its hopeless struggle against the corruption of life itself. The characters become figures of a myth. Life is doom to them as it was to the Greek tragic heroes. We may not accept the myth, any more than we accept Æschylus' view of the Gods of Olympus, but the dramatic power of Anouilh's work is undeniable. With our remoteness from Greek mythology we can see the work of art undisturbed. The philosophy of it is like the hull of a ship – when we are close under it on the sea of time it obscures a clear view of everything above-decks; but when it has receded over the water, then we see the beauty of masts and sails and brave pennons flying, while the hull begins to sink from sight.

The pathetic pessimism of his plays comes from Anouilh's passionate interest in the individual and his deep conviction of humanity's helplessness. Man must despair of ever knowing his true self or his neighbour in a state of purity. We think to escape from loneliness through love; love is a pure emotion and holds out a promise of return to the purity in ourselves that we remember dimly and still feel deep down within the encrustations of our civilised being. Yet the purity of love cannot last, and a whole life's happiness in that purity can be measured in minutes, in seconds – then the decay sets in. We know we are alone, and in a sense we long for our own total loneliness, but we have less and less courage to face it as the years increase our guilt. But suffering is the great badge of man-kind, men are more human when they wear it. Those who through the pure vision of love become suddenly acutely aware of all this are faced with the choice – die, or live a lie. Death is in fact the only pure solution.

The setting for the dramatic conflict is the family, the main source of contact with others; Anouilh shows the purity of the individual in

incessant conflict with family life. He can see no
purity and no beauty in the family, for its values
have stripped love and friendship of all their freshness. The central point of his dramas is the struggle
of the purity in one person's soul against the family,
against friends or even against love, for in all of
them he sees the seed of contamination. In *Le
Voyageur Sans Bagages* Jacques is filled with horror at
the memories his family have of him – he decides
to start life afresh with no family at all, a newborn
adult; in *Le Rendez-vous de Senlis* Georges struggles
to escape from the personality his family and friends
have forced him to adopt; in *La Sauvage* it is the
very presence of her lover that brings Thérèse to
the realisation that their love is impossible.

The other corrupting instrument of society is
money, and in passing it is worth pointing out
how central a theme disgust for money has become
in the best of modern French drama. Jules Romains
and Marcel Pagnol led the attack in the 'twenties and
the fight has raged more or less fiercely ever since,
down to Giraudoux's last play, *La Folle de Chaillot*.
It is a subject that the most diverse writers –
Salacrou, Cocteau, Achard, Pagnol, Neveux,
Bernard-Luc, Puget, Aymé – have in common.
There is not one who does not say his say against
the tyranny of money. But it is in Anouilh that the
money theme has its most serious treatment. For
him riches and poverty are both barriers to the full
realisation of self, and the plays show how love in

particular is continually harassed and wounded by money. Romance says you can escape the evils of money (poverty) by getting rich; Anouilh says you cannot. In *La Sauvage* a rich young man is doomed for ever to be poor in experience, and his fiancée, reared in poverty, finds his riches and his basic ignorance of human suffering both intolerable to her because she has known the humiliations of being poor. This is not to say there is a virtue in poverty, but there is an invaluable experience in suffering. The two young people are incompatible not because of disparity of income but because she, being poor, feels corrupted by all that has been vulgar and vile in that poverty, and the power in his love to expunge that cannot last. In *L'Hermine* the young hero is poor and is in love with an heiress – the drama is in his desperate attempts to procure the money he feels essential to their happiness. "We are poor, Philip," he says hopelessly to his friend. "All those books on morality people write are for us. . . . I'm poor, and I'm stained with the dirt of honest work into the bargain."

Perhaps the most striking money scene of all is in *L'Invitation au Château*. An enormously rich financier offers a large bribe to Isabelle, a penniless ballet-dancer; to satisfy his spoilt daughter's pride he must persuade Isabelle to leave the château. He waves rolls of notes before her eyes, but she refuses them, saying she is leaving in any case but will not have his money. The financier is horrified; he

cannot understand and he is frightened by not being
able to *buy* what he wants. He implores her to
accept. She still refuses. Then the rich man breaks
down; he confesses he has been really happy only
once in his life, when he was young and penniless,
and that in his heart he hates money as much as
Isabelle does herself. For a moment they feel united
in their hatred of money and together tear the
bundles of notes into fragments. They are wildly
excited at this movement of revolt and fall on their
knees together in a spreading carpet of tiny pieces
of paper money. "Away go the holidays abroad,
the servants, the racehorses, the beautiful ladies
ready and willing; away go the consciences of
honest men, and all the prosperity of this lamentable world! There! There! There!" As he tears
up the last note the financier turns to Isabelle and
says: "Are you happy now?" "No. Are you?"
"Not at all," is the pathetic answer.

Poverty and wealth, then, are as cramping as each
other, though poverty has so many attendant
degradations that it is especially hateful. Friendship
and love are both illusory and the soul of mankind
is doomed to despair. The pure in heart must lie
or die; there is no way out, we are all in the trap.
These are the conditions at least of the *Pièces
Noires*, where Anouilh appears to offer little justification for going on living.

The characters of the *Pièces Roses* do not belong
to the same world as those of the *Pièces Noires*, they

are at a much greater distance from reality, for Anouilh treats them in a very special manner.

He is evidently never deceived himself for a moment, but he asks us to pretend to take them seriously and enjoy the way they dart about and perform the most startling antics before he jerks them back off the stage. For the style of their humour is quite set – it is a dramatic ridicule of all who take themselves seriously. But instead of the usual sarcastic ridicule of a serious subject (a technique of which Shaw is the acknowledged master) Anouilh gives us a ludicrously earnest treatment of the most trivial matters. The intrinsic funniness of the earnest fool is brought out, explicit ridicule is unnecessary. It is a method as old as the clowns and more dramatic than Shaw's dialectics. The result is a fantasticated Tchekhov with both the comedy and the pathos of the Russian master in more garish colours.

Anouilh indeed is a most disturbing dramatist, for he deals continually in the unexpected, he is as unpredictable as a shooting-star. No sooner have you adjusted yourself to his poetic phantasy than he will plunge you deep into realism; then as soon as the tears are welling into your eyes you find yourself swept into a burst of laughter. Paradoxically enough this very unexpectedness is part of the inevitability I spoke of above – we sense the same almost divine assurance with which the conjurer draws his rabbits out of the hat.

The great virtues of Anouilh are theatrical virtues. He has a coruscating style, a brilliant gift for pathetic dialogue, a profound respect for emotion, and an unerring sense of comedy. His characters have that mixture of the true and the overdrawn that is the very stuff of the theatre, and they are presented in the warm and confident way that lifts you airily along with them into his dramatically conceived world. In addition he has a most unusual view of the human situation, and there lies in some degree a danger. He is if anything too consistent – his view has hardly changed in twenty years though the emphasis is now entirely different, but he was twenty years of age when his ideas were formed. They were uncommon ideas, and their freshness filled the plays with vigour, but their bloom has gone and the seasons have moved on.

Whatever Anouilh does in the future, whether he moulds his old philosophy still again into new shapes, steps over into other fields of thought, or turns his back on his old ideas to expand his magic gift for comedy, we shall always be looking for a dramatic masterpiece from his pen, for he is one of the natural poets of the theatre.

2

The Plays

TO use the terms of the two opposing categories under which Jean Anouilh has published most of his plays it is evident that his personal vision is more *noir* than *rose*. His major characters are either tied to a sordid family or haunted by an unhappy childhood. They all find it impossible to adapt themselves to the demands of everyday life, and though they sometimes manage to build a semblance of happiness out of the remnants of their hopes they never properly enjoy it. The best of them try to escape from the uncleanliness they feel surrounds them and strive for a pure ideal, but they are condemned to failure. Often enough, when circumstances bring them face to face with a vital choice, they prefer suicide to the unending shame of life as they see it.

With a range of characters like these Anouilh might easily have written tragedies of utter despair, but he is a thorough romantic at heart and by nature full of pity. That is why, whenever he puts pen to paper, in spite of his pessimism he seems to produce a work of tenderness and warmth

3

– his bitterness is turned into nostalgia for innocence, and the storm of passionate revolt dissolves into the clear skies and limpid moonlight of love's young dream. But sometimes this division between his reason and his feelings works in the reverse direction – and what begins as light entertainment slips into dark patches of pathos and poignant moments of tragedy.

Some of Anouilh's extraordinary qualities are difficult to grasp outside the theatre and away from the enchantment of the stage, but others will be quickly apparent to anyone who cares to give the plays close consideration. Of all playwrights of today Anouilh is perhaps most worthy of study – he represents a signpost to a vital aspect of modern man, the signpost of uncertainty and insecurity, of dissatisfaction with the outward conditions of life whatever they be, and of longing for innocence. He has brought lucidity and sanity to the tortured cry for mankind's conscience-striken loneliness that came from Strindberg half a century before. All this has been lying too long unseen by the blinkered realists, whose glaring at the particular has blurred the wider visions of humanity both for themselves and for others.

Literary historians are apt to persuade us that the spirit of one generation is abruptly changed by the next, but in fact progress is a much more piece-meal affair. At any given time we find side by side the yesterday, today and tomorrow of every art

and progress comes from variation in their relative
strength. It is only in the case of fundamental
upheavals like war that we can point to any sudden
break where as soon as the mind is free once more
we are conscious of an entirely different pattern
which may not be due to the war but has been made
clearer by it. There is no doubt that the dominating
feature of our post-war society is a deep feeling of
insecurity that affects the conduct of nations and
individuals alike.

No playwright has ever struck so powerful a note
of insecurity as Jean Anouilh, and he was writing
plays of the same tones twenty years ago when he
first tried his hand at drama – it was too early then,
before the cataclysm of Nazism and war trans-
formed the mental climate of the world. Anouilh
was part of the small, unheeded "tomorrow" of
the drama in the 'thirties, and suddenly after the
war he burst on to an astonished world as the in-
disputable master of "today". Yet his plays have
remained in exactly the same vein, in tone and
pattern, in atmosphere and range of character, in
ideas and technique – there have been develop-
ments in Anouilh but no basic changes.

In this examination of the major plays to date
it is hoped that the reader will come to feel familiar
with the special world of Jean Anouilh. His world
is a dream world, but the reality of a drama is
measured by the truth of its emotions – no limit
is imposed on his invention and fantasy so long as the

dramatist keeps in tune with the emotions of his audience. Whatever form or style they favour great dramatists are all poets.

Titles are throughout, for consistency's sake, left in French. Where English versions have been widely performed the recognised English title is also given. In the descriptions of plot the names and details refer to available English versions. Where there is no well-known version, references are directly from the original plays.

L'HERMINE

Paulette Pax's production of *L'Hermine* at the Théâtre de l'Œuvre in 1932 (Anouilh's first proper production) raised no storm of enthusiasm from the critics, but one or two theatre people saw signs of genius in the play. One of these was Jean-Bernard Luc (then also an aspiring dramatist, now one of France's leading writers of comedy), who immediately wrote to Anouilh and sent one of his own plays for him to read. Anouilh returned it a week later with apologies for a large stain soaked through much of the manuscript – he had, in his own words, accidentally "baptised the play with whisky". He and Jean-Bernard Luc have been close friends ever since and collaborate frequently in films, though neither his fellow-dramatist's admiration nor his own whisky celebrations managed to keep *L'Hermine* on longer than five weeks.

The play is full of revolt against the terrors of poverty and makes us think that Anouilh must have found his own impecunious youth unbearable. The degradation of being without money forms the basic theme of most of the early plays, which are all written in the same violent tone. Anouilh was only twenty-one when he wrote *L'Hermine* and fear of poverty and the suffering it brings with it haunts the pages of the play. To be more exact it is not poverty itself (in the sense of having no money) but the fear of never being sufficiently rich that is the core of the principal character, for we are soon convinced that the hero cannot conceive of happiness without money.

A poor young man, Frantz, loves a young heiress, Monime, and she loves him, but her rich aunt and guardian, an old Duchess, will never agree to the marriage. The only solution Frantz can see is to find plenty of money, elope with Monime and thus for them to find happiness together. He tries to get money from an American industrialist, Bentz, for a scheme he thinks will bring a fortune, but the hard-headed business-man refuses him. Frantz can see nowhere the smallest chance of making the money his dreams are built on, and all around he sees the traps of falsity and degradation to defile the pure white "ermine" of his love. He sinks into despair and fastens on to the most obvious solution – the murder of Monime's aunt, the Duchess. He is obsessed with this idea and one night kills the old lady in cold blood. He answers the police officer's questions quite calmly the following morning, for he is fortified by the conviction that he has killed her for a very good reason – to safeguard his love from the contamination of poverty.

"Our love," he says, "is too beautiful a thing, I expect too much from it, for me to risk that too being sullied by poverty. I'm going to build it round with a barrier of money."

He is on the point of slipping through the fingers of the police when Monime appears. She has never for a moment agreed to this fantastic decision and she tells him angrily how revolted she is. Frantz thereupon breaks down and confesses, Monime's revulsion has shattered his universe. He gives himself up to the police, utterly indifferent to his fate.

The starting-point of the character of Frantz is reminiscent of Raskolnikov – he is young, obsessed with the need for money, and murders an old woman because he argues that she is no good to anybody alive. But Anouilh makes Frantz feel no remorse whatsoever; his values are clear to him, and his action only logical. That logic is upset by the, to him, inexplicable horror he inspires in Monime. Then, and then only – when Monime screams at him: "You horrify me! You killed her for my money!" – does his tremendous pride collapse. His clear arguments in self-justification to his friend – "Money is the only thing that can keep you clear of filth and corruption" – are suddenly transparent and he sees they were merely rationalisations of his desires, easing the way to the satisfaction of his overbearing pride.

The play is curiously unmoving, though there are moments of poignancy that could be very effective if only Frantz had some saving grace that made him a more likeable person. Yet in spite of having little sympathy for him, a reader is very impressed by Frantz's passionate arguments, for *L'Hermine* is already written in Anouilh's persuasive style and contains one or two quite remarkable scenes when we consider that it was written by so young a craftsman. Already we find the strange mixture of the odd and the universal in Anouilh's characters and in spite of Frantz's revolting opinions we feel that much of him is thoroughly human.

Monime is fuller drawn and more human than Frantz. There is a wilful blindness about Frantz to some of the most unquestioned human values that makes him less acceptable – in much of what should be the most moving part of the play he is very difficult to believe at all. The audience sympathises with his horror of poverty but can never support the emotional argument that decides him to build his own wealth on a vicious crime. His plan is inhuman and no conceivable weight of argument will persuade an audience to accept it. His character is therefore emotionally impossible, for he runs counter to basic moral feeling and in explanation offers a string of patently wrong-headed reasons.

JEZABEL

Written immediately after *L'Hermine* in 1932, so far never produced, and not in fact published by Anouilh until 1948, came an extraordinary melodrama, *Jézabel*. The characters and situation in this play are a violent intensification of the story of Frantz – a young man in love with an heiress and unable to escape from poverty.

Jacqueline (his fiancée, the heiress) comes to Marc's house to find out why he is avoiding her. To explain, and drive her away, he shows her his father – a feeble old drunkard, only interested in money and girls – and hints that his mother is worse. Then his mother appears, a revolting, drunken old woman, indescribably degenerate, clutching for all she is worth to the sensuality that means so much to her and that she finds with her latest lover. Now we see why Marc was so full of shame – the lover is a chauffeur employed by Jacqueline's father. He roughly tells his father he feels hounded by the shame of his parents and has no freedom left because of them. "I want to get away. I want to live, do you hear ? I can't live with you two !" In a violent scene of mutual confession and accusation his mother tells Marc of her lustful longings, and he tells her that his violent hatred of women and love dates from the time he found out as a boy that his mother was a wanton slut. The first curtain falls on her screaming at him her conviction that he is the same and has the same insatiable vulgar lusts as herself, and that his hope of a pure love with the sweet and lovely Jacqueline is moonstruck nonsense.

The rest of the play shows how low Marc's mother has sunk – she deliberately serves poisonous mushrooms to her husband, then searches for the money he had hidden from her. The dead man's relatives are called and tell Marc how his father had always suffered from being married to a monster. Now word comes that the chauffeur has left without a word, and the mother is broken-hearted. In a further melodramatic scene Marc learns how she poisoned his father and feels he has tasted shame and degradation to the dregs.

In the final act Marc is preparing to leave, but his mother and the disgustingly venal maid Georgette (who is Marc's mistress and who connived at the murder, for a bribe) are trying to hold him back. Jacqueline appears in a last attempt at persuading him to marry her in spite of her wealth. "I am rich. It's a disgraceful thing to say, I know, but you'll see how easy everything is if only you have the money."

But he is brutal to her, flourishes all his mother's vices in front of her, degrades himself and his origins as much as he can, to hurt her, and finally – when she still begs him to go with her because it is his only chance – he takes his share of the worst infamy of all and pretends that he knew all the time when his mother was serving and preparing the poison. Jacqueline is horrified at this, and goes. In his anger and revulsion Marc had sworn he would not leave his home: "I want to stay here in my own filth where I belong!" But his mother's vulgar blandishments when Jacqueline has left, and Georgette's debauched familiarity, fill him with disgust and he rushes wildly out, leaving the maid to continue her cynical blackmail of his wretched mother.

Jézabel reveals the melodramatic Anouilh. The characters are grossly overdone, there is a frenzied insistence on the horrible and a lack of detachment about the handling of the story. Anouilh could hardly have made a cruder statement of his thesis that man wants purity, cannot be delivered from impurity by himself, and that his very horror of the impurity in his past drives him to hate and reject salvation. How much more delicately and with what dramatic power he was to use this theme and even the main features of those characters again! *Jézabel* is unrelieved melodrama but it may have served to purge the young Anouilh of his most rabid feelings about the visions inspiring those early years of his art. One feels that if he published such a play sixteen years later, when he had moved on so far from what it represented, it must be because it meant a lot to him.

LE BAL DES VOLEURS

The next play is an improbable farce on this same theme of poverty and wealth. It is written with a butterfly lightness of touch and brings merriment and laughter to the problem that had been so tragic to both Frantz in *L'Hermine* and Marc in *Jézabel* – the difference of status between two lovers. The whole play is interwoven with music and dance and makes a charming comedy-ballet that reminds us of Labiche and Molière at their gayest.

Le Bal des Voleurs, though written in 1932, was not produced until six years later. In that summer of 1938 Anouilh was on holiday at Erquy with André Barsacq (who was to make his reputation at the Atelier during the war by producing one Anouilh play after another), and they were planning the production of *Le Bal des Voleurs*. Swept on in an exuberant mood they danced an apache dance across the beach through the crowd of astonished sunbathers, throwing themselves into the characters of this joyous farce. And that is the spirit in which Anouilh wrote *Le Bal des Voleurs*; it is a play where he frankly aims at pure entertainment. He has since admitted that he was trying to write a play for the boulevard public and was modelling himself on Louis Verneuil and Yves Mirande, but the result is as far from the models as it could be. It is a charming, dainty piece of fun, adroit and fantastic, full of totally unreal characters – comic figures manipulated by the author simply for our amusement; we do not take them seriously for a moment.

A trio of robbers is introduced in comic disguises

Opening scene of the Arts Theatre production of *Thieves' Carnival* (*Le Bal des Voleurs*). The thieves arrive in their Spanish Grandee disguise. *Left to right:* John Laurie, Harold Lang, Robin Bailey.

Georges Pitoëff as Gaston in *Le Voyageur Sans Bagages* at Les Mathurins in 1937.

Laurence Payne as Gaston at the Bristol Old Vic, 1951.

so successful that they are all trying to rob each
other, until they realise their mistake. They decide
to make an attempt at robbing a wealthy lady of
her pearls by using their special Spanish Grandee
trick. The wealthy lady is an eccentric English
aristocrat (Lady Hurf) and is explaining to her
friend (Lord Edgard) and her two nieces (Eva and
Juliette) how unspeakably bored she is with life,
when she sees the Spanish Grandees approaching. She
impulsively throws her arms round the leader's
neck, pretending to recognise him as a very old
friend, the Duke of Miraflor, and she promptly
invites them to her villa. She has immediately seen
through their imposture, of course, as she knows
only too well that the Duke is long since dead. At
the villa the robbers enjoy a life of wealth and
luxury for some days, while the youngest of them,
Gustave, and one niece, Juliette, quickly fall in
love. This wild masquerade is not fun for long to
Gustave, for he is genuinely in love and soon sees
the falseness of his position. He decides he cannot
cheat any longer and urges the others to do their
job of thieving and hurry away – he cannot hope to
marry the young heiress if she finds he is a thief
and not a Spanish nobleman, so he will be loyal
to his past, rob her and go.

But Juliette discovers his profession and begs
him to take her with him; she will help him and
become a thief too. Gustave responds to her
unquestioning loyalty and drives off with her, along

with two or three sacks of silver and valuables from the villa. That night, when the others have returned from a ball, for which they were all in fancy dress disguised as "robbers", the whole story comes out. Lady Hurf dismisses the robbers and in the circumstances they think themselves lucky to get away unpunished. Then Gustave, who has thought better of eloping after all, creeps in carrying Juliette, asleep, and puts her down on a couch. He stumbles and wakes her; her aunt is horrified at the prospect of this match and agrees with Gustave that it is impossible, but Juliette is obstinate. When he sees that it is a case of genuine love on both sides Lord Edgard tries to overcome the difficulty by suddenly producing a photograph and throwing his arms round Gustave's neck, shouting "My boy! My boy!", and claiming him as his son who was stolen in infancy. Gustave will not accept this solution, for the sincerity of Juliette's affection has turned him quite honest; he is indignant at the proposal. But Juliette draws him confidently into the garden with her and we know that he will soon be convinced by this radiant and determined young girl. Lady Hurf and Lord Edgard smile sentimentally, pleased at the vision of how happy Juliette will be. Suddenly an unknown man with a beard appears – he is a Scotland Yard detective; Lord Edgard has been expecting him throughout the play and mistaking people for him all the time. Lord Edgard tells the detective he is no longer needed, upon which the man draws a clarinet from his pocket and begins to play (he has been the clarinet-tist in the orchestra, once noticed before). The curtain comes down on a ballet: the robbers in false beards are chased by a band of bearded police-men, all mingling with the other characters in a hilarious dance in which everybody keeps changing beards.

This is obviously a vividly comic transposition of the money theme, but it is worth noting that the dénouement is happy because of the probable acceptance of a lie. There is a strong suggestion that honesty is not the way to happiness. Particularly also is the point made that the success of the match depends on Juliette's belief in love. That is taken to be the key to success in happiness, a thing that Lady Hurf and the older niece, Eva – both of whom are too experienced – find impossible for them:

LADY HURF: My poor Eva, what can you do? There's no way of learning to have faith. The grand and glorious adventure is over for you and me. We both feel quite alone now, like used corks. The game only succeeds for those who play it with every bit of their youth; only in fact because their youth is the game itself. Youth always succeeds.

Apart from one or two lines like this from Lady Hurf and Eva, who represent the jaded experience that is to worry Anouilh in other plays, *Le Bal des Voleurs* is an enchantingly comic stage entertainment.

LA SAUVAGE

Jean Anouilh pursued the attack on social values with much greater success in *La Sauvage* (1934), indisputably one of his most moving plays. It is the drama of a young girl (Thérèse), pure by nature, whose soul has been ravaged by poverty. Her parents are warped by their past misery and their vileness inevitably affects her purity – she cannot shake off the mould from which she comes. She falls in love with a rich, carefree, talented musician (Florent) and he with her, but his past experience will not permit him to break the barriers of pain and suffering that bar his approach to Thérèse's feelings of bitter humiliation. She cannot forget the vile concessions poverty has wrung from her and she is driven to attack Florent just because everything has always been easy for him – family, friendship, career, love, everything. For she stumbles against his confidence at every turn, feeling herself in a foreign country -- everything about him begins to seem hostile to her. This makes her flare with unreasoning resentment and like a wounded animal at bay she hits out wildly, for the satisfaction of wounding him in return.

Thérèse Tarde plays the violin in a fifth-rate band run by her father. Madame Tarde plays the 'cello; Monsieur Tarde the bass; a young heavily-painted girl, Jeannette, the second violin. The pianist is a man named Gosta who has been Madame Tarde's lover for some thirteen years. This liaison is in the process of breaking – Gosta has tired of Madame Tarde and in any case is now in love with Thérèse. Madam Tarde is clearly prepared to trade him Thérèse if she can keep him herself by doing so – it is a heavy price to pay but there are no depths to which she has not sunk before. It is against this wretched background of failure and vicious compromise that Thérèse has always lived.

The man she loves is the exact opposite – a famous composer, a man supremely happy in everything he does. Calm and confident, through success and the comfortable life that has been his since birth, he is a perfect example of untroubled happiness, and above all of genuine decency, for his spirit is equal to his riches, he is unspoilt. He adores Thérèse.

But he finds that all the qualities that would

seem to make him the perfect husband in fact fight against their love. His confident happiness and her deep-felt misery push between them and keep them away from each other.

Thérèse's family and friends are sure she is marrying Florent for money – and they ask her help in their schemes for using the unsuspecting Florent to line their pockets while the going is good. Jeannette eggs her on to make him buy diamonds because "they always fetch a good price afterwards"; her mother tells her to buy the engagement ring from a jeweller who has agreed to allow her a percentage on whatever Florent takes from his shop; her broken-down old father wants a goodbye concert when she leaves the band, where Florent, the maestro, will give his services free and make a lot of money for them all.

This revelation of the way their minds work is horrifying to Thérèse, for she realises that they can only see the sordid side of everything. But to her they show the inevitable division between how she conceives her love and how it appears to the outside world. She knows her love will always have these two sides to it and what terrifies her is the constant fear that they will mingle and that, like everything else in her life, her love will steadily lose its purity.

In Florent's large country house she is surrounded by luxury and ease, but she has brought her father and uses him to try to make Florent conscious of the depths of the past humiliations that have marked her soul for ever. She encourages old Tarde to eat and drink too much, to wallow in the richness of this life and to show all the baseness that is part of her world. Her father himself is mystified at the way her encouragement is followed ,by sudden revulsion.

"That first night at dinner, for instance, I don't mind admitting straight out, I was disgraceful. I had five helpings of *chocolat mousse*. I dropped an anchovy into my glass; I belched. . . . Mind you, it didn't really matter. Each time I cracked a joke and made people laugh with me. But that first day – your old father humbly admits it – that day I might, to some extent, have made you feel ashamed. . . .

Well, what was your attitude during that first dinner ? You laughed uproariously at every mistake I made. It was you who drew everyone's attention to me and egged me on to take a fifth helping of *chocolat mousse*. But that wasn't the worst, you tried to mislead me about the bowl of warm water they brought to the table after the meal. If your fiancé hadn't stepped in I think you'd have let me drink it, you wicked girl, after you'd let me eat the slice of lemon. When that unfortunate belch just slipped out, your fiancé, who is very well brought up, turned his head away; but you just laughed and clapped

your hands as noisily as you could, and shouted:
'Good health, daddy!' . . .''

Florent's friend Hartman tries to stop her, but
she is determined to hurt Florent:

''You revolt me, all of you, with your happiness! Anybody would think there was nothing
else but happiness in the whole wide world!
Well, I want to get away from it! Yes! I don't
want it to get me while I'm still alive and well!
I want to go on being hurt, and suffering, and
screaming. I do! Extraordinary, isn't it? You
can't understand, can you?''

Not content with this she sends privately for her
friend Jeannette and pays her to tell Florent about
her past lovers. Thérèse is infuriated by Florent's
being unmoved by it all and she at last screams at
him that she had a lover when she was only fourteen,
and she spares him none of the horrid details of her
delivering herself of a child in her own room,
crawling about the room in pain and degradation.
She prepares to leave, but as she says goodbye she
sees a tear in Florent's eye and realises that he is
suffering:

''But you're crying! You! . . . Are you crying
because of me? So you *can* cry? . . .
So you're not always happy, either, in spite of
all the beautiful things you have? . . .
. . . Oh, my darling, you're uncertain, too.

You're ashamed, you're hurt ? But you're not really rich, then. . . .

(*She picks a tear off Florent's face with her finger.*)
. . . Look, look at it, shining there on the end of my finger ! What does all the rest matter now that you've paid me with a tear ? . . .

. . . Oh, you must need me, Florent, then I shan't suffer too much. . . ."

And so, because at last Florent has suffered and really needs her, she dismisses her father, symbol of her ignoble past, and stays.

Later, as she is being fitted with her wedding-dress, she seems contented and resigned, and makes no sign of revolt while Florent's aunt and sister talk with the dressmaker and her assistants about charity and the poor and the luck of the working-girl. But Thérèse cannot forget altogether – she calls back the youngest seamstress and in a pathetic aside that the girl cannot understand asks her to forgive her for the expensive wedding-dress that costs as much as the girl can earn in a year's hard work at her sewing.

Hartman congratulates her on her new attitude but she still has some reserves, for she has to force herself continually to accept this "happiness" that she sees and at moments shrinks from in her fortunate in-laws :

THÉRÈSE : . . . I need their kind of warmth now they have taken my own away from me. . . . But it's like being in a play you don't know, being happy like them!

HARTMAN : You must learn your part.

THÉRÈSE : I am learning it, with all my strength. I'm already feeling soaked in gentleness and ease. I don't feel so hard as I was, nor so pure. . . . What you have to do is never give a thought to the others living, struggling, dying as they do. . . . I shall always stay here, and I shall never go out except with them, in their fine trains, waited on by the polite servants in their splendid hotels. . . . I shall let my eyes rest on the things they see and only on them – flowers, precious stones, happy faces. . . . And I shall be confident and lucid, as they are, and never know anything else . . . that must be wonderful, never to know anything else. . . .

But suddenly, to remind her once more, her father comes back – the pianist Gosta has taken to drink and mad with jealousy threatens to kill Florent. In a few moments Gosta appears, hiding a revolver in his pocket. Thérèse goes to him and takes the revolver from him, and he suddenly realises how pointless his anger is. Thérèse turns on him and her father now and begs them to go away :

"Go away, both of you. I want to be happy and never think of you again. You're unhappy, but why should that matter to me ? I've got out of it myself! You're ugly, you're dirty, you're full of nasty thoughts and the rich are quite right to hurry past you in the streets. . . . Go away, go away quickly, so that I never see you again. . . .

Go on! Go away! Can't you see I've had enough and can't carry you in my heart any longer!"

After their departure a dressmaker arrives for a final fitting of a small cape for the wedding, but Thérèse sends her away as Florent comes from the next room, where he has been playing the piano throughout the previous scene. Thérèse has realised that Florent has settled back into his comfortable happiness again, only now she is part of it too. She wistfully talks with him about their honeymoon plans and then asks him to go back to his piano. He does so, kissing her lightly and saying how happy he is, and a minute after he has gone Thérèse says softly:

"You know, Florent, it's no good my trying to cheat and shutting my eyes as tight as I can . . . . There will always be a stray dog somewhere in the world to stop me from being happy."

And as the piano begins to play again beautifully in the next room, she gently pats the wedding-dress hanging over an armchair, then turns roughly away and rushes out into the night. She is convinced that she will be even lonelier with Florent than alone in her own resentment against the corruptions of this world, and runs away from the life of comfort and ease and love that is offered to her, to return to the world where she knows she belongs although it fills her with disgust.

Anouilh has thus reversed the commonplace mill-girl-meets-millionaire story – in *La Sauvage* Thérèse is the one with the full knowledge of life, experienced, disillusioned. He gives us the simplest possible situation – a poor girl and a rich man – drowned in a sea of complication. Facing one another on the brink of marriage each of the lovers makes the other feel first conscious, then guilty of all that has been done and said around them, and they both see each other framed in their past . . . habits, family, past experiences colour their every move and feeling. Inside them are two innocent creatures who could be united in a pure and lasting love – but both are enveloped in a name, a social position, a group of friends, and a past. Not their souls but the memories that the world has irremovably impressed on their souls must always fight against each other and make their deepest wish for ever impossible of realisation.

The tragedy is in Thérèse – it is a tragedy of pride, the pride to which she owes the consciousness of her own worth, the pride that has been the only prop to enable her basic purity to withstand all the compromising and bargaining of her kind of life.

But her suffering is incommunicable to Florent – although he is brought to see that the deeper men's unhappiness the more human they become. But he can do nothing about it, for there fate is against him:

"Tonight I have come to understand that suffering too is a privilege that everybody is not fortunate enough to have."

He discovers that his very happiness is a form of inferiority.

Thérèse's character is one of pure revolt. Reason, inclination and good luck all point the easy way. Against all these she defends her integrity – an integrity wounded but made more sensitive and compassionate by experience. Her sense of what is *fitting* – what sort of happiness she is capable of enjoying and giving – decides her actions. This sense is something pure and fine which is in touch with life at a point beyond considerations of justice and happiness; by it she apprehends a meaning or pattern in life, a purity which has its own laws in relation to each individual soul. The ordinary pursuit of justice and happiness dulls this sense in most people, dulls them to the deeper knowledge of the "fitting". Thérèse preserves it intact. Ordinary notions of happiness are irrelevances. Happiness in any sense is irrelevant. It is only this sense of the purity by which her soul will remain whole that can give life a meaning and direction.

No arguments can save Thérèse from her predicament. Like Antigone in the famous play to come during the German Occupation, she could in full explanation of herself say simply: "I am here to say 'no'!" There is only one thing – love – that might obliterate Thérèse's degradation, and even give her self-respect.

Florent, by a twist of fate, is just the man who is incapable of the love that can transform her. He is too perfect, terrifying in his certainty of happiness – for it seems to be argued that the wretched can understand the happy because of their very knowledge of suffering, but no knowledge of happiness will help to an understanding of pain. Pure happiness in fact is for ever beyond Thérèse's reach.

That is why we can feel so deeply for Thérèse and not reject her as an impossible character – she seems all feeling, totally human, no cold logic or argument holds her together. We judge her, then, as a person, not as a character, and since we feel she is not guilty of her misfortune we must pity her. Even when for the brief moment in the middle of the play she feels she has at last achieved happiness, we know that this is only a further illusion, another lesson she must learn.

Usually young people are so sure they can avoid the mistakes they see others make, so sure they can succeed in spite of earlier failures. Why are Anouilh's young people so pessimistic? There is no reasoned answer. Even in the *Pièces Roses* this is true. They seem to be conscious of a lack of grace, or at least certain that grace is not to be won in life and the pursuit of happiness. Thérèse perhaps will nevertheless find it in life; her play is sad because what she loses seems so good and worthy. If her prospects with Florent were anything less than perfect, the point of her rejecting him would be missed. When Ibsen's Nora leaves her Doll's House we are glad to see her rational wish to be true to her nature fulfilled. When Thérèse leaves Florent for the same wish it is something irrational that drives her on. The conflict is at a deeper level, a metaphysical level.

An extraordinary thing in this as in most of Anouilh's plays is the way the theme and the whole structure of the characters are made to depend on money and yet how thoroughly non-social the play is. The explanation is to be found in the meaning of the terms ''rich'' and ''poor'', ''happy'' and ''unhappy'' as used by Anouilh; they appear to have very special connotations. The whole question of happiness in the early plays in particular is in money – rich means happy, poor means wretched. Rich (happy) means a life of ease and unconcern; poor (unhappy) means insecurity and unceasing humiliation. But it is the pure hazard of this that especially irks Thérèse – she shouts with fury as she faces Florent with her contemptuous accusation against the human condition as a whole: ''You're a rich man, a conqueror who has never had to fight.''

But neither Thérèse nor Florent is in any way

representative of the social divisions of class. No play could be further removed from the sociological play. Nor does Anouilh seem to have any concern for the righteous use of these desirable "riches" he talks of so much – he has no conscience about them, no "cause" to advance, no vision of progress to further. They represent for him entry into a curiously old-fashioned world of country-houses, stables, grooms, butlers and footmen which is always to haunt his plays. Among these outmoded signs of wealth there is some possibility of achieving happiness, but it is still remote, for money as well as liberating the rich also degrades them by the power it gives them to chain others in hopeless slavery.

LE PETIT BONHEUR

In *Le Petit Bonheur*, 1935 (one of the plays he appears to want forgotten), we have a rich young couple, Catherine and Frédéric, whose happy marriage is threatened with disaster because Frédéric is developing into a very different person from what he was. Now that he has more confidence in himself, he is revealed as hard and selfish – and she had been attracted to him precisely because he seemed gentle and she hated violence.

It is her own attentions and encouragement, her tenderness and affection that have given him his new assurance and released the real forces of his brutal temperament which his early training had always kept in check. Frédéric reconsiders his values and decides that self-interest governs the actions of the rest of the world and that the only constant truth in society is the principle of personal profit.

Catherine has loved him so much that she has changed him and at last driven him away. She realises that he is different and does not cling to him, but soon he comes back to her, his personality split in two between his present desires and his memory of the past. He cannot forget her pain at losing him and to ease his conscience has decided that the lesser of the two evils is to settle down as contentedly as he can to a life of ''modest happiness'' with her. But while he is slipping on a dressing-gown, Catherine herself collects her things and leaves, making a final sacrifice to ensure that Frédéric is free.

Revolt and resignation are opposites, as inseparable as two sides of a penny, but up till now Anouilh has shown only the revolt side. This is the first time that we have seen the other side in a clear light and been able to consider what it really means. He must have found that resignation – to the *petit bonheur* – had less dramatic possibilities. At all events it is a long time before he returns to it again, and then in an exuberant mood of satire.

Y AVAIT UN PRISONNIER

Y Avait Un Prisonnier is the story of a man named Ludovic who returns home after fifteen years in jail for fraud. He goes straight from his cell to the yacht in the Mediterranean where his wife, son, father and brother-in-law are waiting for him. They are all fifteen years older, of course, but Ludovic has retained his youth – he appears to have found an advantage in being isolated from his fellows. He discovers that his wife and best friend have degenerated over the years and he lays the blame for this on that very contact with others that was denied him by imprisonment. Society is to blame for their corruption.

But Ludovic is now faced with readjustment and

there is a tremendous stumbling-block – he is too genuine for society. He wants to keep with him another released prisoner, La Brebis, a deaf-mute, and is amazed at his family's opposition. He has just suggested it out of pure kindness of heart, feeling that the first thing any decent man can do is help his fellow in misfortune – but he has to learn the lesson that the more genuine the emotional urge, the more it needs to be controlled. Decency and respectability are two very different things.

Along with this first shock comes the plan for reorganising Ludovic's life to provide him with a living – his father-in-law suggests setting him up in an export business. But Ludovic will not hear of harnessing himself to the machine of daily toil – all he wants to do is try to be happy and concentrate on that. They counter by telling him he must have money to live, and money has to be earned, so he admits defeat. But this is the crucial point in his new development and the formation of his new character, for the amazing truth now dawns on him – his freedom has in fact been stolen from him by the demands of society, he had more freedom in prison than he has out.

On questioning his best friend, Marcellin, a "free" man, about what he did with the last fifteen years he gets a short list of things : a few successful business deals, some travelling, outings with friends, a mistress or two. . . . Ludovic presses him but there is nothing else. So these are the feeble, pointless achievements of "normality" in society – the thing that is prompting them to drive him into conformist slavery too? Ludovic is incensed – but he is also terrified at the thought that he himself might sink into the state of acceptance that he finds so intolerable in the others. If life "at liberty" means that, then he prefers death. So he tries to commit suicide, but is saved by the last-minute intervention of the deaf-mute, La Brebis.

But Ludovic has made up his mind not to compromise with the false values of society – he tells his family that if only they will be honest with themselves and drop this moral hypocrisy he will be reasonable. They are horrified and not one of them is prepared to admit that he is playing society's hypocritical game. Not one shows a sign of sympathy or understanding, so Ludovic sees that it is hopeless. He pulls the deaf-mute with him, climbs over the side of the yacht and swims for shore. As they leap into the sea he shouts his defiance of the hypocrisy he is rejecting.

This is an excellent situation and we can well understand the Hollywood company which so hurriedly bought the film rights of the play. Anouilh did not use it to the best advantage, however, and by making some of the scenes far too long drove his audiences to look for complaint. They found it easily enough in his principal character, for the weakness of the play was in the fact of putting the strictures on society into the mouth of a fairly sordid criminal, pleasant enough in person but nevertheless justly condemned by a not unreasonable law. It was hardly the best way of attacking moral values. Anouilh was not yet skilled enough to sustain so difficult a paradox, original and persuasive as much of the play certainly was. The play was published soon after its production but Anouilh has not included it among his recent volumes of collected works.

LE VOYAGEUR SANS BAGAGES

In the next play the same problem of the individual against society is presented, but Anouilh has found a way of putting the whole of the audience's sympathy on his hero's side. In *Le Voyageur Sans Bagages* (1936) Gaston is a young officer who was found near a prisoner-of-war train in 1918 and had lost his memory. He is the living Unknown Soldier and has been a national enigma for eighteen years. A new psychiatrist at the hospital has decided that Gaston shall visit in turn the six families whose claims to him (after many hundreds have been eliminated) are thought to have equal chances of being substantiated. His contact with them over the several days of a visit should awaken something in his memory about the family where he really belongs.

He comes first to the Renauds' house for the experiment to begin – over the four acts of the play he is concerned with discovering the past of young Jacques Renaud, who he is supposed to be. He interviews the family one by one, sees the brother, the mother, sister-in-law, even the servants, and soon realises how sordid this wealthy, respectable family really is. The mother, full of pride and ill-will, had been unnaturally cruel to young Jacques, the brother had married the girl Jacques loved (but she had promptly become his mistress), Jacques himself had been a vicious youngster, wild and uncontrolled, thoughtless, selfish and irresponsible, and given to violent tempers – in one of which (a jealous quarrel over a housemaid he had seduced) he pushed his best friend down a flight of stairs and broke his back. As they pass before his eyes these memories the others have of Jacques revolt Gaston, for they contain nothing but hatred and bitterness. All he can find in Jacques Renaud's past are records of egoism and cruelty that paint a picture of a perfect little monster.

In a remarkable scene with Madame Renaud he discovers how his mother had quarrelled with

Jacques (over his wanting to marry a mere shop-girl he met at a dance) and how she had not spoken to him for a whole year. A feeling of pity for this dreadful and rebellious boy of eighteen, however misguided, going off to the war lonely and un-wanted, makes him violently rude. The scene brings out Madame Renaud's deepest characteristics, and makes Gaston react to her exactly as young Jacques must have done nearly twenty years before.

GASTON: And I died at the age of eighteen, cheated of the thing I wanted most in the world, because you said it was foolish and refused to speak to me. I lay all night out on the battlefield with my wounds, and I was twice as lonely as the others, because they could at least cry for their mother and think how she would have comforted them.

Pause. Then he suddenly says (as though to himself): It's true, I do despise you.

MME RENAUD (*appalled*): Jacques, you don't mean it!

GASTON (*coming to himself, sees her again*): Hm? Oh! I'm sorry. . . . Forgive me. . . . I'm very sorry. . . . (*He crosses the room.*) I am not Jacques Renaud. I don't recognise a thing that belonged to him in this house and your family. For one moment listening to you, I admit I was confused and did identify myself with him. I hope you'll forgive me for that. But, you see, an entire past is too much for a man to take on all at once, like this. You would be doing me a favour, and I'm sure doing me good, to let me go back to the sanatorium. I've been planting lettuces and polishing floors there, and the days have gone by very peacefully. . . . But eighteen years of that – exactly half, the other half of my life – don't add up to that all-devouring thing you call a "past".

MME RENAUD: Jacques . . .

GASTON: Don't call me Jacques any more, please. He did too much with his youth, that Jacques of yours. Call me Gaston, that's fine: he's nobody, of course, less than nobody, but I do know him. And this Jacques boy, who's surrounded with dead birds and slaughtered animals, who was a liar and a cheat, and maimed his best friend, and went off to the war with not a soul to wave him a friendly goodbye . . . Jacques Renaud, who never loved anybody but himself . . . he frightens me.

MME RENAUD: My poor boy . . .

GASTON: Go away! I'm not your boy!

MME RENAUD: That's the way you always spoke to me before!

GASTON: I've got no "before"! This is the way I'm speaking now! Go away!

MME RENAUD (*stands up stiffly as she must have done always "before"*): All right, Jacques. But when it's been proved beyond a shadow of doubt that you are my son, you'll have to come and ask my forgiveness

(*She goes out. . . .*)

Gaston is revolted by all he hears about the boy, yet he gradually becomes convinced, and finally, when alone with his sister-in-law and former mistress Valentine, has absolute proof (through a scar on his back) that he is the real Jacques Renaud. He is in despair at this, for he has been horrified all the time at the thought of recognising himself in this wretched young boy. But he finds a way of twisting the evidence to his own advantage – he uses it to prove that he properly belongs to one of the other claiming families, the one in which every single member except a boy of thirteen has perished in a shipwreck. Thus he leaves the Renauds for a single relative of thirteen years of age, with no memories whatsoever of the young man who went off to the war eighteen years before – Gaston now in fact has no past, no weight of memory round his neck, no ''baggage'' to burden him on his way.

There is an astonishing strength in the writing of this play – dialogue, characters, use of situation, everything has the mark of a master-hand. We feel him throughout doing exactly what he wants, both with the material and with the audience's emotions. One very famous actor when asked to play the part complained that the second scene in the play gives the whole drama away – this is a short scene in a corridor where the servants cluster round the door, peeping through the keyhole, and saying how sorry they are to see that dreadful Jacques back again, scoundrels like him are better dead, and so on. This actor said it would be better for the audience to learn the truth about Gaston gradually, their horror growing with his increasing revulsion of feeling. As it is the play has no surprise left after that scene, he concluded. Anouilh's significant reply was that dramatists have been telling the audience the story before it takes place since the time of the Greeks.

There is no doubt that *Le Voyageur Sans Bagages* has the stark inevitability of a Greek tragedy : the entire action unrolls with implacable logic in a tone of increasing horror. The only changes made to the formula are Anouilh's comedy and the seemingly happy ending. In fact the ending is a symbolic murder – Gaston "killing" the young Jacques Renaud in order to allow himself to live. Anouilh has written in *Le Voyageur Sans Bagages* a bitter, moving tragedy showing the same rifts in the individual as in *La Sauvage* and *L'Hermine* and giving us the unusual experience of being wholly in sympathy with the murderer as well as with the victim – for the two are one. All his plays are in this sense tragedies – they all kill one or the other of the aspects of personality. Denial of oneself, the bloodless murder. "It's a horrible feeling, killing somebody else just to save your own skin," says Gaston when he decides to deny the evidence and refuse to be Jacques Renaud.

Gaston is free of memory, he is presented as beyond the reach of the past which clamps the other characters of Anouilh in its paralysing grip.

Thus by following Gaston in his search for the truth we feel we are analysing the basis of all character, the elements of individuality. This is another side to the theme of revolt, this time a revolt expressed as it were by the observer rather than the person involved: there is less prejudice and more reason than in the normal way. Gaston is two persons, one of whom is reconstituted before our eyes through the memories of other people—a whole new character is built up by implication through the opinions of others. This is a technique that is very strongly reminiscent of Virginia Woolf in the novel and Pirandello in the theatre – we are left wondering which can possibly be the real Gaston, and whether both are not equally true. Gaston himself begins to see more clearly in Act III:

> "Duties, obligations, hatred, cruelty and malice . . . What was it I used to think memory would be like ? . . . And I always forget remorse. . . . Hm! Now I've got a whole past, packed, labelled and complete. . . ."

This hatred of the limitations imposed on the personality is carried further than ever – the Renauds are a pitifully nasty family group. Anouilh has surrounded this ghostly young man with a collection of sordid, worthless relations – sordid, that is, in relation to Jacques *but quite acceptable* to others. The inference is that any ordinary pleasant family might have skeletons like these bursting its cupboards. Nowhere has Anouilh tried to relieve the oppressive unwholesomeness of this family portrait except perhaps in the pathetic weakness of the brother George. Young Jacques at eighteen went off to the front without a kiss from any of them, and might well have said with André Gide: *"Familles, je vous hais!"* For Gaston's probings reveal only how Jacques Renaud's personality was hamstrung by his family. If he recovered his memory Gaston would have to shoulder all those sordid relationships again; he sees only too well that by acknowledging his past he will lose his freedom. The past is a burden, life is a constant constriction of the self, for we never stop building up these unfinished relationships that are in fact the sum total of ourselves. The past, memory, and therefore life itself that provides the material for memory, is nothing but a self-imposed straitjacket. Gaston with his amnesia is in a unique position, outside the straitjacket – through his eyes we see the incessant frustration to which the individual is condemned.

Anouilh could have weighted his theme in any of several ways – by varying the degrees of wickedness and virtue in Gaston, Jacques and the Renaud family. He chooses perhaps the easiest of them all, he confronts Gaston, the pure and untainted, with a sordid youth and an equally sordid family, and we are not at all surprised when he rejects them. But we cannot help wondering what the drama would have been if Jacques had been revealed as a charming young boy, friendly, imaginative, kind instead of selfish and cruel. Would Gaston have been even more moving confronted by a happy past, like Florent ? As it is he provides a perfect contrast to his experience, like Thérèse. The marriage of the two personalities is as impossible in him as the marriage of the two persons in *La Sauvage*. This conflict makes the drama.

To emphasise this Anouilh even makes Gaston tell us what sort of youngster he would have liked to be – kind and happy, engrossed as a child in innocent toys, shy and rather artistic, deeply attached to a friend whose life he had saved once by risking his own at sea. In his dreams over eighteen years he has built up his lost childhood as infinitely happy, and now the truth – that it was cruel and vicious in the extreme – he finds impossible to believe and his revulsion is almost intolerably moving.

The force of the play is in two aspects of his slow realisation of the truth – the growing horror it arouses in him as he feels he cannot escape the past, and the gentleness and compassion that we feel in Gaston himself. The horror makes him violent, the compassion fills him with sorrow – for there is a generous flow of sympathy hidden in this powerful play which seems to have been written in one of the warmest moments of Anouilh's inspiration.

Anouilh again admits the impossibility of altering

conditions and reality, but here he is content to end on a trick. Instead of sending his hero away into the gloom and hopelessness of despair as he had done in *L'Hermine* and *La Sauvage* he finds a most ingenious way of letting him turn his back on the past and start off with a gay laugh on a fresh trail.

His method of introducing the surprise ending is a masterly piece of comic relief to the tension that Gaston's horror and his rejection of his early self have built up. Gaston, left in despair after a final cruel scene with Valentine in which he has realised that he cannot run away but is caught in a trap, stares at his reflection in the mirror for a moment and then seizes something on the table by him, hurls it at this image of himself, and shatters the mirror to pieces. He drops on to the bed holding his head in his hands. In a few seconds a boy in an Eton suit pokes his head round the door. Gaston looks up and is astonished at this apparition.

BOY : Excuse me, sir. Do you think you could help me ? I'm looking for the place.

GASTON (*coming out of a dream*) : The place ? What place ?

BOY : The place where I can be alone, sir.

GASTON (*understands, looks at the boy, then suddenly bursts out laughing, in spite of himself*) : Well ! Isn't it a small world ? That's just what I'm looking for myself at the moment, the place where I can be alone.

BOY : Oh! well, I wonder who can tell us ?

GASTON (*laughs again*): Yes, I wonder too.

BOY : Anyway you won't have much chance of finding it if you stay here, will you ? (*Suddenly sees the broken glass.*) Oh, dear! Did you break that ?

GASTON : Yes.

BOY : Oh! Well, I can see why you're worried! You know, I think you'd do best to own up straight away. You're grown up, they can't do much to you. They say it's unlucky to break a mirror.

GASTON : So they say.

BOY (*going*): I'll go and see if I can find someone down the passage. . . . As soon as I find out where it is I'll come back and tell you . . . (*Gaston looks at him*) . . . You know: the place we're both looking for.

GASTON (*smiles and calls him back*): Listen, listen. . . . The place you want is much easier to find than the one I'm looking for. Here's one for you, there in the bathroom.

When the boy comes out again Gaston questions him and finds he is from one of the families that claim him. It seems this boy is the only member of the family alive, as all the rest were drowned on a cruise together. Then the solution to his own problem dawns on him – here is a family with no memories of him whatsoever. He takes the boy to the door :

GASTON : We'll go this way.

(*At the door he stops suddenly and asks the boy*) : Tell me, are you quite sure every one of your relatives is dead ?

BOY : Yes. The whole family. And a lot of our best friends. . . . They were invited on the cruise as well.

GASTON : Wonderful !

We feel nevertheless in some degree that Gaston is cheating. We cannot accept his complete denial of his past without a tinge of uneasiness. He is a privileged being and in this he loses a little of our sympathy. We feel that he is not really justified in becoming somebody else – why should he have two chances to everybody else's one ? A reasonable envy colours our content at his escape, to which must be added the oddly disturbing thought – that this dénouement is entirely in keeping with the rebellious and self-centred character of Jacques Renaud.

LE RENDEZ-VOUS DE SENLIS

Georges of *Le Rendez-vous de Senlis* (1937) also breaks with the past and takes it upon himself to build a new life. In *Le Voyageur Sans Bagages* Gaston discovers his family and his own revolting youth and the shock disgusts him so profoundly that he rejects his past; in *Le Rendez-vous de Senlis* Georges flees his real self and family and escapes into the sort of ideal family he has invented in his dreams. There is some sign of hope in this play – it is one of the *Pièces Roses* and describes an imaginary happiness and its near collapse; but it argues that the search for happiness is not bound to fail, if one only has the faith to believe in it whatever the odds. It is built on Anouilh's usual contrast between the dream and reality – and here he has touched a common enough dream indeed, for few of us have not ached at times to be somebody else. This is a thorough *Pièce Rose*, for the dream wins not only morally but also in actual fact. It is the old romantic story of how a dream comes true.

The curtain goes up on a young man and a little old lady going through the inventory of the house he is renting from her in Senlis. Georges is pressed for time and at last declares to the horrified old lady owner of the house that he will sign the documents but will not spend another second checking them, as in seven minutes' time he must be in possession ready to welcome some guests he is expecting on the Paris train.

Who are these guests? Georges has never seen them any more than we have. They are two actors whom he has engaged to play his parents for this one evening, for he plans to entertain the girl he loves as if this were his old home and birthplace. He has also hired the dinner, complete with butler. The table will be laid for five, but his "best friend" (another invention for Isabelle's benefit) will not turn up.

In these circumstances the exposition proceeds on many planes: Georges' explanation, which we feel sure is not the true one; the actors' rôles, which we all know are false; the dream they roughly correspond to in Georges' mind, which to him and Isabelle is real and necessary; and hints of the disillusioned reality behind it all.

Suddenly a message is brought from the house next-door which has a telephone and Georges has to leave at once. He tells the actors to start dinner as soon as Isabelle arrives; he will come back as soon as he can.

With all the pretence prepared, but no Georges, the stage awaits Isabelle as the curtain falls.

The second act is on one plane only. Here we have the distasteful truth. Georges is married to a rich girl, Henriette (never seen in the play), who loves him but whom he has never loved. His parents, his best friend Robert, and Robert's wife, Barbara (who is Georges' mistress), are all parasites on this marriage and have every interest in preventing Georges from breaking it up, however much he may wish to. The scene is in the laundry of the house in Paris. Barbara has slipped away to telephone, but presently Robert and the others join her to get away from Henriette's ravings and threats. As they go over the whole situation, and their prospects if Georges does not return look blacker and blacker, Barbara confesses she knows where Georges is. At this they all rush off in the car to Senlis. Henriette has threatened to throw them all out if Georges is not back by midnight.

From now on the conflict is between Georges' dream of happiness in the future, of which Isabelle is the embodiment, and reality, past and present, compounded of lies, despicable cowardice, and compromise. There are two Georges, Isabelle's and Barbara's. Barbara sympathises with Georges' desire to free himself from his unsavoury past, but it is the unsavoury Georges she loves.

BARBARA : . . . . He's not at all a nice young man, you know, *my* Georges. He's everything you must hate. He's sad, he's never sure of anything. He's unfair, and cruel . . . .

ISABELLE : You're lying.

BARBARA: Oh yes, and he tells lies, too. He's a
dreadful liar. He makes appointments and for-
gets to turn up. He never keeps his promises.
He's petty and mean and makes scenes. You
see, he's a strange man, *my* Georges. . . .

ISABELLE: What good can it do you to run him
down to me?

BARBARA (*smiles*): But that's not running him down.
That's the way I loved him.

The impact of the best friend, Robert, on Isabelle
— the utterly *noir* on the utterly *rose* — is most
dramatic. He is the first to walk in and find her.
The house of cards Georges had built for her had
tumbled when she stepped inside. The actors had
given the game away, collected their fees, and
disappeared. She recognises Georges' "best friend"
at once, but her joy at finding some part of the
story true — Robert does at least exist, and answers
to Georges' description — fades quickly as Robert
comes to understand the position and gives free
rein to his hatred in the most cynical terms. But
his cynicism is always stimulating, his unpleasant-
ness even somehow touching — we treat it patiently,
as though we were faced with a wounded creature
slashing at everything in its pain. This is how
Robert introduces his wife to Isabelle:

ISABELLE (*she has been looking at Barbara for a time;
says softly*): But . . . who are you?

ROBERT (*bows and clowns*): My wife! I don't know

Orpheus and Eurydice
(Dirk Bogarde and Mai
Zetterling) in *Point of
Departure* at the Duke
of York's.

Angus McBean

Angus McBean

Orpheus with his old father (Hugh Griffith) and Monsieur Henri (Stephen Murray).

André Barsacq's sketch for the set of *L'Invitation au Château* at the Atelier.

Houston Roger.

Cecil Trouncer, William Mervyn, Margaret Rutherford, Daphne Newton, and Paul Scofield in Peter Brook's production of the English version (*Ring Round the Moon*) at the Globe, with décor by Oliver Messel.

what I can have been thinking of when she came in. Do forgive me. Allow me to introduce Madame Jeannette Lemoine, known as Barbara because she thinks it sounds posh. Say how-d'ye-do to the lady, now, Barbara. Pay your respects!

ISABELLE: Your wife? . . . But . . .

ROBERT: Oh yes! There's a big BUT! When you scratch a bit below the surface there's always a big BUT in life. Let me give you a tip. Never scratch! It's dangerous! Never, never scratch! Appearances are quite sufficient, they make a whole world in themselves!

At last Georges himself appears, having hurried back from Paris after a stormy interview with his wife. He tells the family that he will come back home with them, but begs for five minutes alone with Isabelle – during which, in a charming and whimsical scene, they pretend to live a whole married life together. Poor Georges, who has now accepted defeat and is beginning to renounce his dream, has some very moving moments in this extraordinarily pathetic scene.

GEORGES: . . . My lovely, radiant Isabelle . . . what a lot of happy grandmothers you must have way back behind you there, in one long line, holding on to each other's skirts – protecting you. (*Pause.*) It may sound funny, but I think I was a little bit in love with those grandmothers of yours as well.

ISABELLE (*softly, after a moment*): In spite of all those other lies, then, Georges, it was true that you were in love with me?

GEORGES: Yes, Isabelle, that was true.

ISABELLE: Then I'm happy, and I don't care about the rest.

GEORGES: You're right. Let's be happy. (*He ponders a moment.*) We always ask too much of life, you know. We begin by wanting a whole lifetime of happiness, then we learn that to have a few stolen years even is wonderful luck. . . . Later we reconcile ourselves to reality and could be satisfied with a single evening. . . . Then suddenly, we've only five minutes left, and we discover that even that is a boundless oasis in the desert, five minutes' happiness!

When the others come back Robert slaps Georges on the shoulder and the blow makes him faint — the act curtain falls on his telling them that Henriette had been so incensed in the quarrel that she shot him in the arm.

In the fourth act Georges recovers and tells them that he has finished with his old life and is going away with Isabelle to begin afresh and live honestly and purely as he has never done before. The others have to recognise their defeat and hurry off back to Paris in the hope of saving something for themselves from the wreck of the marriage. Georges and Isabelle are left (with the bogus mother and father, as the actors have been unable to catch a train back to Paris), and as the sound of the engine fades down the street Isabelle tells him he is free to live now, for the car has taken them all away. His family and the others do not exist any longer : "You are terrifying, Isabelle," he says, and she replies: "I am happy. There's always something terrifying about happiness." And the curtain falls on their going in to a warmed-up dinner, announced by a hired waiter and shared with hired parents. Georges has turned reality away and gone into the dream that they both know is so false.

This play is an instructive mixture of the two veins of Anouilh's writing, for it is possible to separate the characters into two quite distinct sets – the innocent and the corrupt – Georges himself being a composite of the two in whom the corrupt has been dominant up to the present. The minor characters are in Anouilh's usual strongly marked manner and their peculiarities are etched in with some of the most continuously hilarious dialogue that he has achieved. Consider how glorious a part for an actor is Georges' preposterous father, old Delachaume, whose lines are all in this colourful style :

DELACHAUME : . . . In my time men used to deceive their wives, of course, but they went about it a bit more skilfully. It was no more heinous a crime for that. What's your opinion ?

BARBARA : I haven't an opinion.

DELACHAUME : Of course I don't say this boy of
mine is absolutely obliged to deceive Henriette.
. . . Far be it from me to suggest such a thing!
But what I can't understand about you young
people is this taste for crudity you all have. You
say you like clear-cut situations. So we old people
think : "Good! They're going to put themselves
into clear-cut situations. They're going to behave
as we old 'uns never knew how to behave." But
nothing of the kind! Nothing of the kind!
You're men just the same as we were, and you
get into exactly the same old difficulties, old as
the world itself. . . . Only you're different, oh
yes! You turn your behinds square to the rest
of the world and you think that makes the
situation clear-cut! . . .

   . . . I can't understand this youngster of mine.
He has a lovely wife madly in love with him,
and she's rich. What more does he want?
Answer me that.

ROBERT : What more does he want? Answer him that.

BARBARA : I wouldn't know.

ROBERT : She wouldn't know.

DELACHAUME (*continues*): A mistress? I've told you
what I think about that. Simply a question of
tact . . . Well, what else does he want?

ROBERT (*to Barbara*): What else?

   (*Barbara shakes her head*)

DELACHAUME (*continues*). Nothing. There *is* nothing

else. Money, love, you can't want anything else. Life's very simple after all, dammit! I don't understand you people. He says he's unhappy. Why is he unhappy? Take me, I'm an unsuccessful old artist . . . a failure, and I've had a hard life. But am I unhappy? . . . Well, then? He says he doesn't love his wife. Neither did I love my wife. Did I make such a fuss, just because of that? . . .

And he rattles amusingly on through the acts. *Le Rendez-vous de Senlis* contains some of the most comical moments of all Anouilh's many scenes of inspired humour.

The pathos of the play is built on Georges' overwhelming desire to give himself at least one evening of pure *rose*, all his nostalgia for purity is to be expressed in a few hours of pretence, and then back to sordid reality once again. He is deeply in love with Isabelle and this love makes him feel confident of himself though at the same time ashamed of everything connected with his past – the vile bargains he has made with life are revealed for what they are, stripped of their excuses, disgusting in their naked greed. Anxious not to lose this glimpse of the ultimate values that Isabelle has given him, he invents an entirely new personality for himself, though we realise that the whole fabric of his lies is so feeble that the merest breath of truth will blow it away. This breath of truth is enough in fact to shift the whole tone of the play from *rose* to *noir* in a way that Anouilh had never done hitherto. From the opening of the second act we are swinging from one to the other all the time, for through much of the play Anouilh allows his two styles to run side by side. The worst part of Georges' real life is his friend Robert, who seems to cast a shadow even over the resplendent purity of Isabelle.

In spite of the successful blending of the two types, nowhere in the whole of Anouilh's work is it so clear that his *rose* and *noir* are two diametrically opposed conceptions and that they belong to two entirely different worlds. Georges is driven to escape reality because he finds compromise at last intolerable – and he has to will himself into another character, another set of experiences, in effect another world . . . the world of romantic imagination. His dream is a youthful dream of escape to innocence when faced with the brutal bargainings that adult life must bring. This romantic part of Anouilh's work is an adolescent's daydream – gay, frivolous, delightfully irresponsible, charming in its freshness and invention but nevertheless a daydream, no solider, though more poetically expressed than the average musical comedy. Anouilh's genius makes this daydream enchanting; it is only on reflection that its youthfulness stands out. *Le Rendez-vous de Senlis* is a powerful play chiefly because Georges' authentic background is so real in contrast to the dream.

The contrast between Robert and Isabelle is very disturbing, the more so because they seem to have no effect whatsoever on each other – sharply opposed characters, they are finished and complete before the play begins. Anouilh pulls the strings to make his marionettes work, with the hope that we will share his interest and enjoyment. The sails are set for a cruise into the romantic seas of hope at the end of the play, for Georges has simply dismissed the *noir* side of his life from his mind. The only escape again, as for the more fortunately placed Gaston in *Le Voyageur Sans Bagages*, is in denial, turning his back on reality and advancing into the world of fancy.

The play appears to end happily with Georges trying to find a new faith in love (''I think I shall teach him happiness,'' says the ever-confident Isabelle). There is hope but it is a very limited type of hope. Closing your eyes to the distasteful aspects of existence is at best a temporary measure, and one feels no doubt whatsoever that in a very short time reality will catch up with Georges again and the whole problem will still be there for him to solve. In fact he has dodged the issue, though like Thérèse (and Antigone later) he carries us with him when he says ''No'' to impurity. We sympathise with his feelings though we do not wholly support his move. His counterpart, Thérèse, in *La Sauvage*, difficult though she is, turned her back on the *rose* to plunge back into the *noir* because she could not wholly forget human suffering – it was a generous, not a selfish move and she is much more likely to carry our sympathy along with her. Thérèse refused to save herself, Georges rejects his family and frankly saves himself. Both these decisions leave us exactly where we were – full of nostalgia for purity and happiness, full of the guilt and shame of reality, but no nearer to reconciling one with the other. We feel that this is another beginning, but that in a way cheats us of an end. However, because of Anouilh's skill we give way to the romantic pull of Georges' belief that his love for a pure young girl has washed him clean of the dirt of past experience.

LEOCADIA

In the next play, *Léocadia* (1939), we see almost a reversal of *Le Rendez-vous de Senlis*; instead of an experienced man burdened with guilt, we have an innocent young man loaded with a set of romantic memories of which he must rid himself if he is to achieve happiness. This is a pure romantic comedy, a play about love in an unreal world of phantasy. Anouilh's ingenuity is strained to the utmost to make the characters have even dramatic reality for the greater part of the play. It is questionable if he succeeds.

A young Prince is obsessed by the memory of three days he spent infatuated by a beautiful actress, Léocadia. Léocadia strangled herself one evening as she put on her scarf – she did everything passionately, and on this occasion seized her scarf, tied it far too tight, and died. Her death is described very casually and is as comic and extravagant as most of the incidentals of this strange play. The Prince's aunt, a Duchess, collects in the castle grounds all the material things connected with those three days of adulation and gives them to her nephew – she buys him the nightclub where he drank champagne with Léocadia, the orchestra that played the waltz he danced with her and cannot forget, the *café terrasse* where they drank together, the taxi they drove in, the park bench they sat on, and the ice-cream cart that passed by as they dined. The Duchess also hires a little milliner (Amanda) to play the part of Léocadia and help her nephew to live his dream. The young Amanda quickly revolts against the falsity and pointlessness of this pretence and the Prince after a struggle is drawn away from the ghost of Léocadia by the charm of reality in the person of Amanda.

From the first moment we are in a world of phantasy and we realise that Anouilh is playing with his characters and with us. The play therefore craves our indulgence from the start as a piece of pure entertainment. A serious note creeps in here and there and upsets the mood, for we have less sympathy for these incredible characters the further away they are from the opening tone of sheer extravagance. The play is too artificial, or rather not artificial enough in the right mood – the first mood – to be wholly successful. Here for once Anouilh plays fast and loose with us – we begin to feel the shame and embarrassment of pretence in the same degree as Amanda herself, who begins the game willingly enough but later realises how silly it all is.

There are some charming moments in the play but there are also too many lengthy meanderings with little dramatic justification.

The particular interest of *Léocadia* is rather in its position in the pattern of Anouilh's work as a whole. It is not one of his most successful plays artistically but it is one of the most significant, personally. For it marks the first appearance of a realistic solution to the problem of the romantic dreams of youth. Once again it presents the conflict between the dream world and reality, but here reality is finally the more desirable and the more friendly – the dream is palpably false and stupid, cold and forbidding. In *Léocadia* reality triumphs and the dream is justly shattered. It is a decisive victory – the victory of reality in fact means a rejection of the impossible and an acceptance of the real world.

Anouilh before had always been unwilling to admit that sordid reality could be sane. Only the dream had any validity for him until then, the real was corrupting and totally unacceptable.

EURYDICE

In direct contrast to this light-hearted phantasy came *Eurydice*, the first Anouilh play written during the war (it is dated 1941). It is a parable of the futility and sordidness of life, with all the elements of Greek tragic inevitability – the advance of the destruction of the two lovers is inexorable. It is a harrowing story of two people swept into a strong and perfect love but incapable of retaining and protecting the purity of their passion. We grow every moment more deeply aware of the doom in their relationship – they are too happy in each other, disillusion and tragedy are bound to come.

In this powerful play of life and love at death-grips with each other Anouilh succeeded in charging the trivial with significance in some of the most poignant dialogue he had ever written. The play is a modern restatement of the Greek myth of Orpheus and Eurydice. The son of a penniless musician meets in a provincial railway-station buffet the daughter of an actress in a fifth-rate touring company. They fall in love on sight and go off together. They consummate their love in a shabby hotel. But the dream is broken (like Georges' dream in *Le Rendez-vous de Senlis*) by a sudden return to reality – the touring company manager, who had forced Eurydice to be his mistress, has tracked her down and sends her a note, thereby reminding her of the past. She is filled with shame and she takes the first bus out of the town – the bus crashes and she is killed.

A mysterious stranger, M. Henri, whom they met for a few seconds in the station buffet, appears in the hotel and takes Orpheus to meet Eurydice, risen from the shades, in a dream-like station buffet as before. Only Orpheus is not to look at Eurydice – his love can be saved only if he does not turn his eyes upon it. But Orpheus does look – his love for Eurydice is an idealist love and brooks no con-ditions, so he demands every detail of her earthly life, for he must know the truth. He will not

listen to her protestations of love, he must learn
the absolute truth for himself – so he turns to gaze
upon her and Eurydice has to return to the dead.

Afterwards, back in the hotel bedroom, he is
broken with grief. But his old father talks about
how you must face life's imperfections, take life
as it is if it is to be lived at all. Orpheus will not
make any compromise, for his mind is full of the
perfection of his love for Eurydice. He appeals to
M. Henri, who is the messenger of Death – and
he follows his advice, going calmly on to face his
own death in a wood outside the town, there to
join his ideal for eternity. In the original French
play (but not when it was played in London under
the title of *Point of Departure*) the final curtain comes
down on a short scene of barely a minute where
the lights change in the dingy bedroom and Eurydice
enters slowly. She speaks to M. Henri, who has
not moved since Orpheus walked out to meet his
death, and asks if Orpheus is coming to her. When
M. Henri says he will not be long she wants to
know whether "it" will hurt him – "Did it hurt
you?" asks M. Henri quietly in reply. She then
asks whether Orpheus when he comes will be able
to look at her this time. "Yes – now he will,"
answers M. Henri, "without fear of losing you."
Orpheus appears and they run into each other's
arms. The waiter, who cannot see them, fusses with
the bed, the father wakes up and looks round,
anxiously asking for Orpheus. "Where is he?

Answer me, for God's sake, answer me!'' he cries. M. Henri points to the couple deep in their embrace – but they are invisible to the father: ''Orpheus is with Eurydice at last!''

This very poetic story resets the famous myth and uses it for a sorrowful comment on the condition of man. Men are born to entertain hopeless aspirations, says Anouilh in effect, for they are eternally damned by the impossibility of reconciling the baseness of everyday life with the grander qualities of their minds.

The scenes of lyrical love are matched with visions of life defiled and corrupted – several shades of reality and poetry are blended in the play to show the impermanence of any state of purity. The sordid characters of the first scene are at moments transfigured by the lyricism of love, by the poetry of their aspirations. But reality imposes its values when friends and families bring forward their claims on the lovers. Orpheus and Eurydice each have only one parent – he a father and she a mother – but even that is too much family. The parents are both examples of the compromises essential to continued living and present caricatures of Orpheus and Eurydice – they are symbols of the depths to which they will unavoidably sink themselves. They cannot pursue their love unless they totally renounce the ties of family and friends.

Eurydice has in any case sunk much of the way already, but we are prepared to forgive her sins because they were prompted by kindness – she fell from generosity, she said yes to save another. But she has been soiled in spite of her motive, she is marked with the taint of compromise – evil cannot be undone, the stain is ineradicable. Like all Anouilh's characters she and Orpheus have not enough confidence in love, the glare of truth is too strong. They suffer like the Greek tragic heroes who measured their strength against the gods, only in Anouilh the gods have become the conscience itself, the memory of things done in the past. Eurydice would like to rewrite the past, but she has to see that there is no escape from memory.

EURYDICE : . . . Are you sure we can't sort out the bad characters and just keep the good ones ?

ORPHEUS : Too good to be true ! . . . Impossible. They belong to the past now, the good and the bad alike. They have done their little turn, said their little say in your life. There they are – with you for ever.

(Silence)

EURYDICE : Well, suppose you've seen a whole lot of ugly things in your life ? Do they all remain with you ?

ORPHEUS : Yes.

EURYDICE : All lined up, side by side, all the dirty things you've seen, all the people, even those you hated, even those you ran away from ? Do you think all the sad words you have heard remain deep down inside you ? . . . You are sure that even the words you have said without wanting to, and could never take back, are still on your lips when you speak ?

ORPHEUS : But of course, my stupid.

EURYDICE : . . . But then with all these things around, you are never alone. You are never sincere even when you want to be with all your heart. If all the words are there, and all the smutty laughter, if all the hands that have touched you are still glued to your skin, then you can never become somebody else ? . . .

Orpheus is an idealist who by definition is denied the right to look his loved one fully in the face. If he does look her in the face he will lose her. Orpheus tries to look not only into Eurydice's face but deep into the recesses of her heart – for his kind of love can never know enough of the beloved. But the lover soon gets lost between the true and the false, and in the end it is knowing that kills love. The truth brings separation and despair, lies alone can bring harmony and hope. M. Henri explains to Orpheus how death is preferable to life :

M. HENRI : There is only one good thing about death, and nobody knows what it is. Death is good, frighteningly good, afraid of tears and suffering. And when possible, if life permits, death is swift. Death soothes, unravels, and gives release ; whereas life is obstinate, clinging on like

The Mexican Tango scene from *Ring Round the Moon* with Marjorie Stewart as Lady India and Richard Wattis as Patrice Bombelles.

Illustrated

Illustrated

Millionaire Messerschmann (Cecil Trouncer) tears up banknotes with the help of Isabelle (Claire Bloom).

The two children (Lance Secretan, Angela Foulds) dressed up for playing "mothers-and-fathers" in the London production of *Ardèle* at the Vaudeville.

Denis de Marney

Denis de Marney

(*Below*) Mary Morgan and Jacques Castelot as the Countess and the Count in *Ardèle* at the Comédie des Champs-Elysées.

a pauper even when foiled, even when a man can move no more, is disfigured or doomed to suffer without end. Only death is a friend, with a finger giving back features to the disfigured, bringing peace to the damned. Death is the deliverer.

ORPHEUS (*suddenly shouts*): But I would have preferred Eurydice disfigured, suffering, old!

M. HENRI (*his head drooping, suddenly overcome*): Of course, another doubter. You are all alike. . . . Who was she exactly, the little Eurydice you thought you could love?

ORPHEUS: Whoever she is, I still love her. I want to see her again. Give her back to me again, however imperfect. I want to be hurt and ashamed because of her. I want to lose her again and find her again. I want to hate her and soothe her afterwards like a child. I want to fight, I want to suffer, I want to accept . . . I want to live!

But when he does see Eurydice again on the dark station platform he begins to realise that he was asking the impossible, digging into her heart for the truth:

EURYDICE: The day will break soon, darling; you will be able to look at me then.

ORPHEUS (*shouts suddenly*): Yes, one look into the depths of your eyes, as into deep water. Head first into the depths of your eyes. I would like to rest there, and drown.

EURYDICE: Yes, darling.

ORPHEUS: For in the long run to be two is unbearable. Two skins, two impenetrable sheaths round us, each of us on our own, each quite shut in, do what we will, with our own air, our own blood, all alone in this bag of skin. We hold one another tight, we touch one another to get ever so little beyond that terrifying solitude. We have a little pleasure, a little illusion, but soon we are quite alone again with our livers, our guts, and these are our only friends. . . .

EURYDICE: Do not speak any more. Do not think any more. Let your hand move about me. Let it be happy alone. All would become so easy again if you'd just let your hand love me and not speak any more. . . . Be willing to be happy, please. . . . Be willing if you love me.

ORPHEUS: I can't.

EURYDICE: Then at least be quiet; don't say anything.

ORPHEUS: I can't do that either. Not all the words have been spoken yet and we must speak all the words, one by one. We must go on to the very end. . . .

. . . Now I have got to look at you.

EURYDICE (*flinging herself against him*): Oh, wait, do wait, please. We must wait till the night is out. It will be morning soon.

ORPHEUS: It is too long to wait for morning. It is too long to wait till we are old.

EURYDICE (*holding her arms round him, her head against his back, imploringly*): Oh, please, please, darling, don't turn round, don't look at me. What is the good? Let me live. . . . I may not be the woman you wanted me to be. The one your happiness invented that wonderful first day. . . . I shall give you all the happiness I can. But don't ask of me more than I can give. Be content. Do not look at me. Let me live. . . .

ORPHEUS (*shouting*): Live, live! Like your mother and her lover, maybe, with their cooing and their simpering and self-indulgence; then the fine meals, and afterwards they make love and everything is all right. Oh no. I love you too much to live.

Orpheus cannot keep his ideal and have the truth as well, but the need for truth is the stronger and he looks at her and sends her back to death, kills his ideal. To emphasise the justice of this decision the mysterious M. Henri tells Orpheus what would have happened if she had not gone back:

ORPHEUS: . . . I am not the kind to find his own consolation from evil in saying: "That's life." What does it matter to me, d'you think, that it's life; that a million other grains of sand are crushed at the same time as I?

M. HENRI: They are your brothers, as they say.

ORPHEUS: I hate them all, every one of them, so let nobody come and try to make of their million sorrows a big sister of compassion for me. Each of us is alone. Each is quite alone. That is the one thing certain.

M. HENRI (*leaning towards him*): And you, then, you are alone because you have lost Eurydice. Don't forget what it was life had in store for you, that life you found so dear. It was that one day you would find yourself alone side by side with a living Eurydice.

ORPHEUS: No!

M. HENRI: Yes. One day or other. In one year, in five, in ten if you like, perhaps then without ceasing to love her you would notice you didn't want Eurydice any more, and Eurydice didn't want you either.

ORPHEUS: No!

M. HENRI: Yes, it would have been as humdrum as that.

Their beautiful love would have foundered and sunk and all that was left when they had ''accepted'' life would have filled them with disgust. M. Henri cynically uses Orpheus' father to show him the outrageous decay to which life would have brought them:

M. HENRI: Come on, get up, go with your father. The fine career of those who live is still before you.

(*This he has said more bitterly, leaning over Orpheus. Orpheus raises his head and looks at him.*)

Jean Anouilh

FATHER (*after a pause, still engrossed in his cigar*): You know, my lad, I have been in love, too.

M. HENRI: You hear that, he has loved too. Look at him.

FATHER: That's right. Look at me. No need to tell me it brings sadness. I have suffered too. I'm not even alluding to your mother. When she died we hadn't been in love for quite a time. But I lost one woman I adored. A creature of fire from Toulouse. Carried off in a week. Bronchitis. I howled like a dog in the funeral procession. I had to be helped into a café. Yet look at me now.

M. HENRI (*gently*): That's right. Look at him.

FATHER: . . . What is past is past. Life is here. We've jolly well got to live it, haven't we? . . .

M. HENRI (*bending over Orpheus*): Life is here, life is here, Orpheus. Listen to your father. . . .

FATHER (*seated and blowing like a porpoise*): It's a question of will. Everything in life is a question of will. That's what always got me out of the worst fixes. My will-power. A will of iron. . . . Ah, my boy, life is wonderful! . . . And the man who is talking to you has suffered. Drunk life to the very dregs. He often kept silent, bit his lip till the blood flowed, to stifle the moans. His companions of the festive board little dreamed the torture he sometimes went through. . . . Betrayal, scorn, injustice. . . . You sometimes wonder why my back is bent and my hair prematurely white. If you only knew how heavily life lies on a man's shoulders . . .

(*He pulls at the cigar without success, looks vexed, and flings it away with a sigh. M. Henri goes up to him and holds out his cigar-case.*)

M. HENRI : Another cigar ?

FATHER : Thank you. I'm ashamed. Yes, really ashamed. What an aroma! The band is a little beauty. You know, my dear sir, I've actually been told that the girls who make these roll them on their naked thighs. . . . (*He sighs.*) On their naked thighs. . . . (*He stops.*) What was I saying ? . . .

M. HENRI : If you knew how heavily life lies on a man's shoulders . . .

FATHER (*nipping off the end of the cigar with his teeth*) : Yes, yes, that's right. If you only knew, my boy, how heavily life lies on a man's shoulders. (*He stops, takes a long time lighting his cigar, and concludes simply*) : It is very heavy indeed, my boy, extremely heavy. (*Unctuously he takes a long draw at the cigar.*) Marvellous! (*He winks at M. Henri.*) Gives me the impression I'm smoking her thigh! (*He tries to laugh but chokes with the smoke.*)

So in his turn Orpheus decides to die. Life will tolerate only lies and he will not hide the truth, he insists on facing it. To live means inevitably to compromise the truth, to pile shame on shame – death is the only solution. M. Henri's arguments prevail :

ORPHEUS: . . . I don't want to die. I hate death.

M. HENRI (*gently*): You are unjust. Why hate it? Death is beautiful. Only death offers love its true climate. You heard your father speaking about life just now. Grotesque, wasn't it? Lamentable? Well, that was life. That buffoonery, that futile melodrama, is life . . . yes, that heaviness, that play-acting is really it. . . . It is an immaculate Eurydice I am offering you, a Eurydice of the genuine features that life would never have given you.

And Orpheus joins Eurydice in the only place where they can really belong fully to each other – in death it will be easy for them both.

Life is a hollow farce if it is taken at its proper value, but Orpheus, like his brother and sister idealists in the previous plays, carries in his mind a vision of absolute perfection and cannot compromise. Suicide is the noblest step he can take, for only in death can lovers keep eternal faith.

Jean Anouilh was not writing propaganda for general suicide in *Eurydice*. He was writing his interpretation of a famous myth, trying in that way to present a poetic vision of those who pursue the ideal and will be content with nothing less. Just because he is one of them Orpheus must of necessity choose death, for life maintains incessant war on the ideal. Instead of accepting life and hoping for

grace Anouilh's heroes all aim hopelessly at purity.
Death is the only solution – and each play is a
modified dissertation on the values of life and
death.

Anouilh is deeply aware of the tragedy implicit
in the very condition of man. In *Eurydice* he
puts words of compassion for humanity into the
mouth of one of his satirical characters – Vincent,
the broken-down, defeated actor, talking to
Eurydice's mother, romancing for all he is worth,
as false a person at this moment and as bad an actor
as he has ever been:

VINCENT: Oh, love, love! You see, my sweet, on
this earth where everything crushes us, where all
things deceive and hurt, what a wonderful comfort to think there still remains to us – love. . . .

MOTHER: My great big pussy-cat. . . .

VINCENT: Men are liars, Lucienne. Hypocrites,
fickle, false . . . babblers, bombastic and base,
vile or filled with lust; the women – inquisitive,
treacherous, artificial, vain or depraved. The
world an unplumbed cess-pool, its formless,
crawling creatures wriggling over mountains of
filth. But in this world there is one thing holy,
sublime – two beings, loathsome, imperfect,
merging into one.

MOTHER: Yes, darling. That's from *Perdican*.

VINCENT: Is it really? I've played the part so often.

In this way the speech is made hollow and ridiculous

and Anouilh forces out of us a patronising smile for the absurdity of such sentiments as these.

This is an example of one of the principal features of Anouilh's technique – continual incongruity. Anouilh has a double gift, for he has as deep a sense of the comic as he has of the tragic and as pure a flow of romantic lyricism as he has of startling realism. His peculiar contribution to the theatre is to have discovered a style of dialogue and drama where he can mix his tones and his effects as freely as he chooses. It is the quality of this mixture that constitutes his extraordinary theatrical talent – Tchekhov alone among dramatists has blended the comic and the poignant to so powerful a degree.

Yet in *Eurydice* there is perhaps something a little too contrived. The parallel with the Greek myth is too strained to carry the weight required of it – the two characters are dwarfed by their ghostly namesakes, their symbols reduce them rather than increase their stature. There is a danger of the story sinking into a sort of frame supporting a morality tale, for the "human" qualities of Orpheus' father are in fact not nauseating at all – they hardly seem to justify Orpheus' momentous decision. "If only his name were not Orpheus!" you find yourself thinking.

It may be that what at first seems to be a virtue is in fact a weakness – we find ourselves continually trying to read a deeper significance into the dialogue simply because we are aware of the classical parallel.

It appears to be an unfair advantage Anouilh is using to force us to concentrate: he is jogging our elbows all the time, telling us the characters are not really what they seem. It is curiously disturbing to have to face a signpost in bold letters saying this story of two doomed lovers represents the hopes and aspirations, the suffering and despair of the youth of all time.

ORESTE

In 1945 Anouilh published in *La Table Ronde* a fragment of an Orestes drama which he probably came to regard as a sort of trial run for *Antigone*. In its one short act the similarity to *Antigone* is clear. Ægisthus, who succeeded Agamemnon, is a realist, a man of calm resignation, who tries to dissuade Orestes from revenging his father Agamemnon; he tells him what an intolerable load of guilt the murderer must bear. He persuades him that there are other and better ways of proving one's manhood and taking the measure of life.

But when the fragment ends we are beginning to realise that Agamemnon's daughter, Electra, is a perfect Anouilh incorruptible. She could never tolerate an understanding between Ægisthus and Orestes, for she is the kind who will doggedly humiliate herself with the sole aim of feeding her hatred and keeping alive her craving for vengeance. Had this play been completed it could have led to scenes very closely parallel to some of the most famous scenes in *Antigone*. But Antigone has a better case than Electra; it would be difficult to sustain a modern play on the morality of revenge. This one act has very powerful characters, of which the most impressive is Ægisthus, who bears a close resemblance in every way to Creon. It has not, of course, been produced. and its publication no doubt came two or three years after it was written.

ANTIGONE

Anouilh's second wartime play was not produced until February 1944, in the last six months of the

German Occupation, when tempers on both sides were rising and every play was discovered to contain some measure of allusion to the national situation. The *Antigone* plot of personal loyalties in conflict with the demands of authority was as close as any subject could be to the problem of the moment for so many Frenchmen. Anouilh's play was a centre of dispute : some saw in it a clear demand for revolt against authority, others thought is was a justification of "Vichyism". Whatever the political allusions in the play, in most other countries of the world where the emotions of Occupied France were not in any way involved Anouilh's *Antigone* has been recognised as a major work. It is, as Gabriel Marcel called it on the occasion of a recent Paris revival, a "witness-play", that sets before the bar of humanity a picture of the whole inevitable degeneration that living in this world must incur.

Anouilh's Antigone cannot accept men as they are, and she is driven to die by her total incapacity to tolerate the demands of life. Like the Antigone of Sophocles, but for different reasons, she could say :

"... There is no punishment
Can rob me of my honourable death."

The bones of the story are the same as in Sophocles. Œdipus' two sons, Eteocles and Polynices, have killed each other in battle outside the walls of Thebes. King Creon orders a splendid funeral for Eteocles, who was protecting the city, and Polynices' body to be left for the carrion to pick on the battlefield because an example must be made of him as a traitor. It is proclaimed that anyone who dares to perform the funeral rites over Polynices will be punished with death. Antigone defies this ban and scatters earth over her brother's body. She is caught and taken to Creon, who tries to save her by showing her how stupid and pointless her defiance is. She refuses to accept his arguments and goes willingly to death. Hæmon, Creon's son and Antigone's fiancé, curses his father and kills himself in the tomb where Creon has walled up Antigone. On hearing this Eurydice, Creon's wife, cuts her throat in grief and the wretched Creon is left to lament and wait for death alone.

Into his play Anouilh seems to have distilled all his own basic themes – Antigone becomes the symbol of purity of personal conscience, she asks too much of life, she is youthful idealism personified. She will not learn from experience and refuses to give way.

This is the only Anouilh play where the two sides of the conflict of life and death are properly developed into an argument. In the others the scales are so heavily weighted that the issue can never be in doubt. In *Antigone* Anouilh has so strengthened the opposition in the person of Creon that even Antigone herself begins to waver and we are never sure of ourselves for long.

Anouilh wrote the play to be given in modern

dress – the clothes (evening dress for Antigone, Creon, and the Chorus) and the numerous anachronisms (Eteocles is said to have driven a motor-car, the Queen to have "put down her knitting . . . gone up to her lavender-scented room, with its embroidered doilies and its pictures framed in plush") are clearly intended to bring the play as close as possible to our own time. The anachronisms are not used for cheap comedy, but they do have a startling effect at moments in the play. It is debatable whether any real purpose is served by them, for they are often enough an embarrassing hurdle for the audience to clear. The same aim inspired *Macbeth* in khaki uniforms and Sam Brownes, but it is now generally admitted that this makes little addition to the force of the story.

The great virtue of this play is in the magnificent central scene, where Creon and Antigone gradually reveal the basic motives of their conduct. The scene is really in two main parts: the first is almost a replica of Sophocles, where Antigone asserts her loyalty to her brother whom she held in affection, and her determination not to deny him the traditional funeral rites, and where Creon declares his authority which he will not allow her to flout; the second part is pure Anouilh, where the Greek values are no longer in dispute and ruler and rebel go deeply into the reasons for accepting or rejecting life on its own terms.

At the opening of this central scene Creon tells

Antigone to go to her room and he will hush up her defiance of his edict, but she says : "Why ? You know I shall only do it again tonight . . . ." Then she gives her reasons, the usual ones for traditional burial and her loyalty to her brother. She adds that she knows the consequences and feels sure Creon will put her to death. Creon is taken by surprise at this, but then accuses her of having the same pride as her father Œdipus :

CREON : . . . Your father was like that. For him as for you human happiness was meaningless ; and mere human misery was not enough to satisfy his passion for torment. . . . You come of people for whom the human vestment is a kind of straitjacket : it cracks at the seams. You spend your lives wriggling to get out of it. Nothing less than a cosy tea-party with death and destiny will quench your thirst.

Antigone still disdains his orders. He shifts his ground and gives his cynical view of the burial ceremony — surely Antigone does not believe in all that sham ?

CREON : Tell me, Antigone, do you believe all that flummery about religious burial ? Do you really believe that a so-called shade of your brother is condemned to wander for ever homeless if a little earth is not flung on his corpse to the accompaniment of some priestly abracadabra ? Have you ever listened to the priests of Thebes when they were mumbling their formula? Have you ever watched those dreary bureaucrats while they were preparing the dead for burial – skipping half the gestures required by the ritual, swallowing half their words, hustling the dead into their graves out of fear that they might be late for lunch?

ANTIGONE: Yes, I've seen all that.

CREON: And did you never say to yourself as you watched them, that if someone you really loved lay under the shuffling, mumbling ministrations of the priests, you would scream aloud and beg the priests to leave the dead in peace?

ANTIGONE: Yes, I've thought all that.

CREON: And you still insist on being put to death – merely because I refuse to let your brother go out with that grotesque passport; because I refuse his body the wretched consolation of that mass-production jibber-jabber, which you would have been the first to be embarrassed by if I had allowed it? The whole thing is absurd!

ANTIGONE: Yes, it's absurd.

CREON: Then why, Antigone, why? For whose sake? For the sake of them that believe in it? To raise them against me?

ANTIGONE: No.

CREON: For whom then if not for them and not for Polynices either?

ANTIGONE: For nobody. For myself.

E. Brücken

Jean Anouilh with André Barsacq in the studio of the Théâtre de l'Atelier.

Jean Anouilh discussing a point with the cast of *Ardèle*, on stage at the Comédie des Champs - Elysées.
Left to right: Claude Sainval, Mary Morgan, Marcel Pérès, Jean Anouilh, Andrée Clément, Jacques Castelot.

B. M. Bernand

Angus McBean

The antagonists Creon and Antigone: (*left*) Jean Davy and Monelle Valentin in the Paris production; (*right*) George Relph and Vivien Leigh in London.

This is the turning-point in the scene and in the play. Here Anouilh's Antigone gives us her exact position. There is no more pretence about great loyalties or eternal values. From this point on the subject of the play is the temperament of Antigone and the practical expediency of Creon's edict. Creon explains how circumstances forced him to act as he did. He found he had to accept responsibility one day and he would have felt a coward had he refused. The job had to be done, so he said yes. Antigone will not accept his argument and says he should have said no; there is no reason at all for accepting anything you do not want, you can always refuse, she says.

CREON: But God in Heaven! Won't you try to understand me! I'm trying hard enough to understand you! There had to be one man who said yes! Somebody had to agree to captain the ship. She had sprung a hundred leaks; she was loaded to the water-line with crime, ignorance, poverty. The wheel was swinging with the wind. The crew refused to work and were looting the cargo. The officers were building a raft, ready to slip overboard and desert the ship. The mast was splitting, the wind was howling, the sails were beginning to rip. Every man-jack on board was about to drown — and only because the only thing they thought of was their own skins and their cheap little day-to-day traffic. Was that a time, do you think, for playing with words like yes and no? Was that a time for a man to be weighing the pros and cons, wondering if he wasn't going to pay too dearly later on; if he wasn't going to lose his life, or his family, or his touch with other men? You grab the wheel, you right the ship in the face of a mountain of water. You shout an order and if one man refuses to obey, you shoot straight into the mob. Into the mob, I say! The beast as nameless as the wave that crashes down upon your deck; as nameless as the whipping wind. The thing that drops when you shoot may be someone who poured you a drink the night before; but it has no name. And you, braced at the wheel, you have no name, either. Nothing has a name – except the ship, and the storm. (*A pause as he looks at her.*) Now do you understand?

ANTIGONE: I am not here to understand. That's all very well for you. I am here to say no to you, and die.

CREON: It is easy to say no.

ANTIGONE: Not always.

CREON: It is easy to say no. To say yes, you have to sweat and roll up your sleeves and plunge both hands into life up to the elbows. It is easy to say no, even if saying no means death. All you have to do is to sit still and wait. Wait to go on living; wait to be killed. That is the coward's part. *No* is one of your man-made words. Can you imagine a world in which trees say *no* to the sap? In which beasts say *no* to hunger or to propagation? Animals are good, simple, tough. They move in droves, nudging one another onwards, all travelling the same road. Some of them keel over, but the rest go on; no matter how many fall by the wayside, there are always those few left which go on bringing their young into the world, travelling the same road with the same obstinate will, unchanged from those who went before.

ANTIGONE: Animals, eh, Creon! What a king you could be if only men were animals!

Creon comes again to the attack, this time the fiercest blow of all – he tells Antigone that Polynices, the brother for whom she is risking death, was a wastrel and a traitor, and that Eteocles was as bad, there was nothing to choose between them. In any case when the battle was over they were both so mutilated that they were unrecognisable; Creon picked one body to bury and left the other to rot – he does not know and does not care which was which.

So Antigone's gesture of loyalty is ridiculous in the extreme – it has no reasonable justification, it is utterly senseless.

This devastates Antigone and she agrees to go to her room. Before this she had vaguely tried to assert an ultimate value – justice: her gesture had

not been entirely without point. But Creon now
makes the mistake of patronising her and offering
advice, giving her his view of social life and the
way to achieve happiness. Immediately, instead of
admiring his practical approach, Antigone sees the
deep reasons for her opposition to Creon – now the
feelings that prompted her are clear.

ANTIGONE : I spit on your happiness ! I spit on your
idea of life – that life must go on, come what
may. You are all like dogs that lick everything
they smell. You with your promise of a humdrum happiness – provided a person doesn't ask
too much of life. I want everything of life, I do ;
and I want it now ! I want it total, complete,
otherwise I reject it ! I will *not* be moderate. I
will *not* be satisfied with the bit of cake you offer
me if I promise to be a good little girl. I want
to be sure of everything this very day ; sure that
everything will be as beautiful as when I was a
little girl. If not, I want to die !

What she wanted to do was say *no* to life and to
the people like Creon who were prepared to live it
with all its inevitable corruption. She had seized
this edict of Creon's as a pretext for a gesture she
would have had to make sooner or later. His
acceptance of false values is shameful and no one
is obliged to accept shame, one can always refuse.
That in fact is what she is doing – she is refusing
life, for she will not renounce the noble absolutes

that are in her aspirations (and in Creon's, as he has admitted by his apologetic explanations) just for this wretched bribe of "happiness". In her view happiness is the price of capitulation.

In the last analysis Creon is the one who is unhappy – he is the one without faith, not Antigone. He feels this, and shows that he is even ashamed of the arguments he is using, though his obstinacy is itself pathetic throughout the disasters that befall him at the end of the play. Many of his lines have a haunting nobility about them, the more poignant in that his kind of temperament is more common among us than is Antigone's.

In spite of their opposition to each other, both she and Creon have given in – Antigone by her refusal to live and Creon by the manner in which he frames his acceptance. They cancel each other out – each one justifies the other, and each contains a lot of the eternal features of mankind.

One of the most moving parts of the play is in the brilliant Guard scene when Antigone is waiting to be walled into the tomb. Here Anouilh says in a most dramatic manner that the purity of an emotion depends as much on the person who reports it as on the one who feels it. The uncouth Guard's grotesque repetition of Antigone's final message to Hæmon is a travesty of the love and purity it expresses; they are unavoidably sullied by his unworthiness. Antigone herself is suddenly overwhelmed by the realisation of her essential loneliness as she looks at the Guard and measures how completely alien he is to her and how far she must be from the mass of humanity. "I don't know any longer why I'm dying," is her pathetic admission, but it is capped by one of Anouilh's peculiarly tragi-comic lines from the insensitive Guard: "Nobody ever knows why he's dying."

What is most disturbing is the apparent pointlessness of Antigone's sacrifice. It is referred to again and again, the Chorus at the end even saying: " . . . if it had not been for Antigone, it's true, they would all have been at peace," Her gesture of defiance is thoroughly gratuitous: she says *no* to life *a priori* – she has no need to wait for time to prove her right, she knows it all.

Anouilh wrote in *Antigone* neither a play of character nor a play of the conflict of ideas, but a mixture of both. He has not got the best out of both in this way, but the blend is now and then arresting. The characters of Antigone and Creon do not in fact permit of a properly developed conflict of ideas, for neither is faced with a substantial opponent; they merely offer each other a flat contradiction. The discussion is limited by Anouilh's characterisation. Antigone's lack of justification (her view of life is based on instinct, not on experience – she does not draw on the past like Thérèse in *La Sauvage* or Georges in *Le Rendez-vous de Senlis*) is a dramatic weakness, though it is an obvious development from the characters who rejected life because of their experience of degradation. Creon on the other hand goes further than simple acceptance, for he has resolved his emotional problems by ignoring them altogether.

Yet we all have both Creon and Antigone within us. For the only reply that can shame Creon's excuses is the reply from youth, the one his own youth would have made, a reply whose innocence he has actually experienced and remembers with regret. "Sooner or later there comes a day of sorrow in each man's life when he must cease to be a child and take up the burden of manhood," he says to his son. Conscience is mainly the memory of innocence. We have no conscience when we are innocent; only afterwards do we realise what we have lost and try to a greater or lesser degree to act in faithfulness to it.

The whole play balances on the point of a pin — sometimes the point is so tiny as to vanish altogether, so unreasonable is Antigone's resistance. But if the point of a pin is blunted, you throw the pin away. It is no good giving way and breaking faith with innocence on one matter, merely because it seems too tenuous, and thinking you can still make a brave stand when a bigger issue arises. Once you have given way you are blunted. No wonder the *Résistance* felt that Antigone was on their side! Death is not always the result of such a stand but it is always the logic of it. Every idealist is a potential martyr. But martyrs are rare and the rest of us are so well acquainted with Creon's arguments that they find echoes in every heart. His is the voice of reason, experience, and a philosophic acceptance of life. It is all so estimable and right – no wonder many people thought that Vichy had found a spokesman!

Whether we sympathise with Antigone or Creon, or both, the play carries us on with the same dramatic force. Though we probably feel more pity for Creon (and with him all mankind) than for Antigone. We feel for her because she is a helpless, lonely child, but her purity and pride are sufficient to themselves. Anouilh's brilliance is in making us see the problem in these terms: the pride and purity of the death-wishers, the pitiful condition of those who seem to grow up, and accept.

The appeal of the play is to be found in the sense of solitude in all men that Anouilh has so poignantly conveyed. No defiant little youngster in any nursery, or later faced with the world of men, ever felt more lonely than Antigone as her Guard walks her away to death; and no aged statesman ever looked more futile than the broken Creon as he leans on his page at the end of the play and gives his final view with a bitter smile ·

CREON: . . . In a hurry to grow up, aren't you?
PAGE: Oh yes, sir.
CREON: I shouldn't be if I were you. Never grow up if you can help it.

ROMEO ET JEANNETTE

"I don't want to grow up," says Jeannette, Anouilh's next heroine, in *Roméo et Jeannette* (1945). Furthermore she means exactly what Antigone meant in the previous play – "I don't want to say yes," she goes on, "everything is too ugly." She is another of Anouilh's sensitive and rebellious heroines, but she is the second to be impure. She is like Eurydice, the opposite of the intransigent Antigone who has had and will have no truck with the world of reality. Jeannette has already compromised – that is her tragedy, like Eurydice's, for the brand of love that comes to her is beyond compromise. Antigone could not face the future, Jeannette cannot tolerate the past.

Roméo et Jeannette, as the title suggests, is the story of a pair of modern lovers who are gripped by an all-consuming passion. The Jeannette of the title is clearly meant to bring the grandeur of the classic love-story down to more commonplace levels. What's in a name? Jeannette is an aspect of Juliet. Her great love comes to a similar disaster – the double suicide of herself and her lover, stricken with despair by the contrast between what they feel their love could be and what surrounding reality

121

makes it. In this play Anouilh has unhesitatingly
mixed strident comedy and romantic drama in the
Shakespearian manner and it is remarkable how
reminiscent some of the moments in the play
appear to be simply because of this jumbling of
tones. The mixture is perhaps not wholly successful, for it is difficult now and then to accept the
pessimistic romanticism of the lovers in the bitterly
comic background that sets the tone of the play.

Julia, a quiet, pleasant girl, teacher in a small
private school, brings her fiancé Frédéric, a stodgy
young solicitor, and her future mother-in-law, a
rigid conventional bourgeoise, to her home on the
Breton coast. Very much against her will she has
agreed that Frédéric shall meet her father and
make formal request for her hand. All three look
thoroughly respectable as they walk on to the stage
when the curtain goes up – in complete contrast
to the shockingly untidy room in which they find
themselves. Although Julia has given plenty of
warning and even sent money to make certain of a
proper meal being ready when they arrive, it is soon
only too clear that no preparations whatsoever have
been made to welcome them. There was no one
to meet their train, there is nothing at all in the
kitchen, there is no one in the house – no sign of
either Julia's father, sister or brother. The mother-
in-law is furious and decides to walk back to the
village and buy some food. A moment after she has
gone out Lucien appears, Julia's brother. Lucien

is young but his wife ran away from him some two years before, one day when she said she was going out to buy a pair of gloves. He cannot forget this and is permanently embittered – the word "cuckold" is constantly on his lips and infidelity and treachery forever in his thoughts. His scorching cynicism and his bitterness go with a strong sense of poker-faced mockery; he quickly goes to his room before Julia's plain displeasure at the affront they have offered to her in-laws and when he returns later he has put on his father's tail coat (which does not fit him) in their honour.

Julia's down-at-heel father now appears loaded with food parcels, for he has met Frédéric's mother in the village. He is an easy-going, incurably indolent drunkard who wanders on aimlessly through life reclining in comfort, smoking a cigar, drinking good wine whenever he can, talking wisely at the least opportunity only to say the exact opposite with complete unconcern as soon as it suits him. (The London production of the play, *Fading Mansions*, at the Duchess Theatre in 1949, transferred the action to Ireland. The father fitted admirably into this new setting.) He wastes his time as thoroughly as Lucien, and Julia presses them to explain how they have managed to eat in the last few months, since she has been unable to help them out of her modest salary. The last shameful item is soon brutally admitted by Lucien – the mainstay of the family is Jeannette, a violent, defiant sister, wayward and sluttish to an extreme, who has taken Azarias, a wealthy local man, for her lover, to earn the money that has kept the family going. Lucien is quite unperturbed by this, considering it as a matter of course. The father is satisfied with a comic gesture of mixed dignity and impotence: when Lucien calmly states that everybody knows the facts about Jeannette's virtual prostitution, he leans back on the sofa, puffs at his cigar, and says grandly: "I beg your pardon. *I* do not know them." Julia's horror is the final emphasis on her difference from her family – she has managed to escape from a hopeless environment and now does not fit at all.

Julia wants to rush away but her future mother-in-law suddenly appears with a chicken she has found and killed in the garden for their lunch. A moment or two later Jeannette rushes in, indignant about the slaughter of her favourite cockerel, "Léon". She rails violently at Frédéric's mother, saying Léon was a sensitive bird who must have suffered horribly and known it was Death coming to him behind the hideous features of this cruel woman. Frédéric is as if paralysed by this weird and turbulent woman – and we sense that a sudden flaming passion has been born between this stolid, respectable solicitor and this wild slut of a girl.

In the second act, that evening, both Jeannette herself and her cynical brother try to persuade Frédéric to forget Jeannette and to be sensible and marry Julia. But he will not listen. Jeannette, only too willing for her arguments to be rejected, agrees to go away with him. He tells Julia and she heaps insults on Jeannette, telling all her shameful secrets. The lovers simply walk out of the house hand in hand in spite of the warnings from Lucien about God hating happiness and always being on the watch to tear love to pieces. As they go the father, who has been asleep on the sofa throughout, wakes up with a jump and enquires goodnaturedly: "Well, children, how is it? Is it all over now?" "It will be very soon," answers Lucien, looking after the two lovers who have walked out through the French windows. "Very soon. It's just begun."

The third act brings us to the great love scene in a small hut in the woods, but we see clearly within a few minutes that this irresistible love is doomed to misunderstanding. There is a disturbing lyricism in this scene that does not seem to spring from joy at all but from a sense of doom and desolation. The utter improbability of love at first sight between a provincial solicitor and so wild and unconventional a girl spoils the dramatic power of the characters. The scene is tedious, for the lightweight characters Anouilh has prepared for it cannot carry it through. The climax of the scene is in a paltry fib Jeannette tells to explain why she has a ball-dress, a white gown she says at first she bought second-hand with money saved from selling wild duck eggs. Then she changes the story – she had ordered it from Paris on money from pawning the family silver. Her stories are too ridiculous and Frédéric does not believe her. On Lucien's appearance it is all cleared up – her lover Azarias sends word that she can keep the dress if she likes. Frédéric is mortified to find it is a present from her lover, but softens towards her again when she breaks a window-pane and cuts her arm with a piece of glass to prove she will be faithful to him. Then the news comes that Julia has tried to commit suicide, and Frédéric, who had been clearly conscious all the time of the pain he was causing his fianceé, rushes back to her. The act closes with the crushed and wounded Jeannette opening the door to Azarias, who has been waiting about outside all the time – "You may come in now," she says.

Back in the house in Act 4 some days later can be heard the music coming from Azarias' château where Jeannette is being married without a single member of her family present. She has arranged the music so that it will be heard by them all and especially by the man who betrayed her by having no faith. Frédéric is in fact preparing to leave with Julia, who has recovered from the dose of poison she took in her despair. But Jeannette now comes in in her white bridal gown and offers to die with Frédéric if they cannot live together. He refuses roughly and she goes. The others go out to the car in order to catch their train back to town, but when he is already in the car Frédéric sees Jeannette walking out on the shore into the sea. Life itself means nothing to her now without him – the world to her is "well lost for love". The father describes the scene excitedly from the living-room window as it happens: Frédéric has jumped out of the car and is pushing on through the rising tide to Jeannette's side; he speaks to her, puts his arm round her, and they stand there together until both are swallowed up by the waves. Lucien takes this double tragedy calmly and bitterly, accepts it as part of the Almighty's design, which he has despaired of ever coming to understand.

So the two great princely lovers of Verona are reduced to modern squalor and prostitution in order to bring out yet once more Anouilh's basic theme of the hypocrisies and compromises essential to everyday life. But *Roméo et Jeannette* is not a pæon of romantic love. We do not feel – as we do after *Romeo and Juliet* – that their love was greater than life itself, and that real love is in fact stronger than death. Yet Anouilh's title is no pointless parody but an exact signpost to the calculated, almost venomous attack on romantic values that the play is meant to be. The two sisters' names, Julia and Jeannette, mixed make "Juliet", and it seems to me that Anouilh chose them deliberately to represent the two halves of the ideal, with neither of which could a man be content, and which only too justifiably are both loved by Frédéric.

The first two acts are brilliantly written and provide some of the most extravagantly comic dialogue in the modern theatre, but the long love scene is one of Anouilh's least successful, for the characters begin to over-explain. The secondary characters are broadly sketched as usual and are amazingly real – from the mocking and hopeless father to the confident and indignant mother-in-law. The talkative, continuously tipsy Lucien steals the play, but he, like everyone else, is too odd to have more than a limited appeal. The play would be more tragic if the lovers were not so ill-assorted; and the ending might seem more justified if the things that impede their love were less trivial. The hero and heroine are not close enough to win our sympathy and not noble and remote enough to prompt our admiration.

Though he has made his lovers too improbable to matter to us, Anouilh has put another quality into this play which is new for him and which from this point forward assumes a great importance in his work – the quality of pity for the common failings of humanity. As before, love and happiness, purity and perfection are vain dreams, but a hint of new values offers compensation. At certain moments we sense a warm resignation, almost serenity, that has its centre in the bitter and resentful Lucien. His poignant disbelief, but also his inexplicable moments of faith, stay a long time in the mind. He does not believe in love and happiness, but he has flashes of belief in other kinds of joy; he is in fact the reverse of the usual Anouilh principal

The chorus (Sir Laurence Olivier) introduces the characters and the play in the Old Vic production of *Antigone*.

Antigone (Monelle Valentin) dictates to the soldier her last message for her fiancé Hæmon —Théâtre de l'Atelier.

André Barsacq's sketch for the love-scene in *Roméo et Jeannette*.

André Barsacq's sketch of a backstage corridor and dressing-room for the first act set of *Colombe*.

character, for he has said goodbye to hope and youth and accepts life as it comes. Sentiments of this nature creep even into Frédéric's speeches; he says, for instance, in reply to Jeannette's protest quoted above:

"We must grow old; we must some day grow up and out of our childish world; we must accept the fact that everything isn't really as wonderful as when we were young."

Lucien gives his variant on this theme by saying it is in any case futile to protest:

"Die . . . die. . . . Dying is nothing. Start by trying to live; that's not so much fun, and it takes longer to do."

Anouilh meant his audience to feel that maturity brings a decline into failure and misery – all because of some maleficent power that rules over our destinies. From the very beginning Anouilh has been preoccupied with purity and justice, corruption and the sense of sin, without reference to God. Here he paints a picture of a cruel God who is quite indifferent to humanity except in one respect – he cannot tolerate human love and happiness. Lucien's curses at the impossibility of love in this world are frightening in their intensity. He cannot let an opportunity go by:

"Everything good is prohibited on this earth, didn't you know that? . . . That chap up there . . . every time he sees anybody happy it puts him in a terrible rage. He doesn't like it at all."

Later he expands this:

"It's so easy to be happy. There are formulæ for it, and mankind has spent centuries working them out and perfecting them. Cheat, my dear fellow; cheat everything and everybody, and especially yourself. It's the only way you'll get that chap up there to leave you in peace. He's got a weakness for people who cheat – either that or he's shortsighted, or he's fast asleep!"

But malevolent fate in this play is far too arbitrary for us to take very seriously. Nevertheless the play shows Anouilh now prepared to consider the human condition in the round and not simply rail against it, with his heroes and heroines, because life is too difficult for the pure in heart. Life considered as the acceptance of its own limitations is a new realisation to him and this gradually shows in the characters that from this point take over and dominate the Anouilh world. But worldly injustice still dazzles him and in *Roméo et Jeannette* he gets no further than this slight shift of ground. So far it is still a revolt, against the fact that the impure compromisers get the pickings of what this world has to offer:

"God shows a marked preference for people who cheat and compromise, with life, money and social conventions."

This bitter view is summed up in the defiant indifference with which Lucien accepts the suicide of Jeannette and Frédéric and hurries off to Africa to get away from man-made society. As the couple drown he mockingly fills up his glass with wine and says:

"Pardon me, Lord, but you make me feel thirsty."

MEDEE

There followed in 1946 what can only be a rarely produced play but one which is important in the development of Anouilh, for it is in the nature of a second *Jézabel*, which early in this chapter I went so far as to call a purge. As *Jézabel* freed Anouilh of the extreme violence of his feelings against the degradation of poverty and allowed him to develop that theme with more control and more art in the next few years of his writing, so did *Médée* serve to clear away, it seems to me, the last remnants of his obsession with death. For his version of the Medea story contains both an attack on the passionate values of the justifiably but insanely vengeful Medea, and a corresponding statement on the part of Jason that he has finished with vain longings for loyalty and pure love and that what he wants now is to come to terms with life.

The play is a tragedy in one act, which follows broadly the same lines as Euripides except that Anouilh makes Medea, after murdering her two sons, burn herself and them in the flames before Jason's eyes as the play ends. It is not a very successful play dramatically and its chief interest lies in the fact that Anouilh here for the first time casts doubt on the virtue of rebellion, asserts that the constant refusal of other people's values is a vain attack on humanity, and admits that there is a lot to be said after all for resigning yourself to compromise and accepting life without resistance.

JASON : I loved your black world, your daring, your revolt, your conniving with horror and death, your rage to destroy. I believed with you that we had never to stop taking, and fighting, and that no holds were barred.

MEDEA: And you don't believe that tonight any more?

JASON: No. I want to accept now.

MEDEA (*murmurs*): Accept?

JASON: I want to be humble. I want this world, this chaos through which you led me and held my hand – I want it to have some proper shape at last. There's no doubt you are right – that there's no rhyme or reason to it, no light, no rest, that we ought to go on groping with our blood-stained hands, strangling everything, throwing away what stays in our grasp. But I want to halt now, and be a man. Perhaps without any illusions either, like the people we used to despise – I want to do what my father and my father's father did, and all those people who, before us, and more simply than we have done, consented to clear a small piece of ground for man to stand on in the darkness and confusion of this world.

So it is not always the young and hopeful and inexperienced who cry Revolt! Our sympathy flies all the more readily to Jason because Medea is such a monster. He is a calmer and more rational hero than Anouilh has ever had:

JASON: . . . I'm not young enough to suffer now. I answer all those appalling contradictions now, all those insoluble problems and the suffering and the pain, with the simplest gesture man has discovered to help him live: I sweep them aside. . . . I accept what I can see as fiercely and as resolutely as I rejected it all before, when we were together.

And when Medea at last kills herself, triumphantly shouting that he will never forget her:

MEDEA: Now try to forget me! (*She stabs herself and falls into the flames. . . .*)

JASON: Yes, I shall forget you. Yes, I shall live. And tomorrow, in spite of the blood you left behind after you had been at my side I shall start building up again my wretched little human framework beneath the indifferent eye of the powers that be.

Now it is Jason, a man who accepts this impure world until the day that death comes to deliver him, upon whom the light of interest and sympathy is trained. This complete change marks a vital stage in Anouilh's attitude.

L'INVITATION AU CHATEAU

In *L'Invitation au Château* (written 1946) Anouilh
set out confessedly to write a *comédie d'intrigue*. It
is somewhere between the extravagant farce of
Le Bal des Voleurs and the disturbing mixture of
grave and gay in *Le Rendez-vous de Senlis*. More
people in England have seen the play (in Christopher
Fry's adaptation *Ring Round the Moon*) than any
other play by Anouilh. Critics and public in Paris
and London alike were enchanted by this exquis-
itely mannered theatrical conceit. Beverley Baxter
in his notice grandly castigated three unnamed
gentlemen who came away from the first night and
said they did not like *Ring Round the Moon*: "To be
able to walk with wit and keep the common touch,
to be charmed to a tear and still remember that it
is foggy outside, to touch the moon with your hand
and yet think of food rationing, to drink champagne
and still realise that water is the natural quencher of
thirst . . . like the Roundheads in the Civil War
such men are right but repulsive." By common
consent this Anouilh play is an entrancing entertainment – a fantasticated fairy-tale decked in
wit, elegance, extravagant but tasteful comedy,
and some moments of arresting but gentle irony.

It is a tenuous artificial comedy – at one moment
like an intellectual skit on the cheap love-story, at
the next like a grotesque *commedia dell'arte*, at still
another like a symbolic ballet. But it is also a
fascinating treatment in the gayest possible vein of
many of Anouilh's usual gallery of characters and
themes.

A pair of handsome aristocratic twins, identical
in looks, poles apart in temperament, live in a
château with their aunt, Madame Desmermortes.
One twin, Hugo, is furious at his brother Frédéric's
engagement to a rich girl called Diana who really
loves him, Hugo, but is marrying Frédéric out of
pique at being rebuffed. So Hugo brings to the
betrothal ball Isabelle, a beautiful young dancer;
his plan is for her to steal the limelight by her
beauty and the mystery that Hugo's whispering
campaign will create around her. The little dancer
may be penniless but she is not without spirit and
turns out not quite so obedient as Hugo had hoped.
The infuriated Diana spreads the rumour that
Isabelle is not a real guest and seizes the first
opportunity to attack her. Frédéric appears as they
are fighting, Isabelle thinks he is Hugo and all her
disgust for the conspiracy streams out. Frédéric is
touched at this genuine distress and for the first
time takes his eyes off his fiancée and looks at the
girl. A sudden interest grows between them.
Diana's multi-millionaire father, Messerschmann,
offers Isabelle a fortune if she will leave, but she

refuses it – she is quite determined by now to leave in any case. After various complications and some highly fantastic and amusing scenes with minor characters, Isabelle and Frédéric, of course, come together and Hugo turns to Diana at last.

Anouilh's success in this sophisticated farce is in a class by itself, for this play of extravagant gaiety somehow leaves a touch of uneasiness in the mind. Its improbable characters here and there touch a deep chord that sounds long after the gaiety has dimmed and gone. Much of the brilliance of the play is in the leaping, imaginative dialogue and the extraordinary grotesqueness of the characters. Anouilh appears to have taken all his favourite puppets out of the box and given them a garish coat of paint: Isabelle's sweetness and injured innocence remind us powerfully of the heroine (Isabelle again) of *Le Rendez-vous de Senlis* and particularly of Amanda in *Léocadia*; the twin's aunt we have often glimpsed before – as Lady Hurf in *Le Bal des Voleurs*, as the extravagant Duchess in *Le Voyageur Sans Bagages*, or even as far back as *Humulus le Muet*; Isabelle's mother is a sillier edition of Eurydice's; Frédéric in his single-minded purity is like one aspect of all Anouilh's heroes and heroines, Hugo in his mocking bitterness is like the other aspect of them all, when their purity has been soured by experience. The complete contrast between Hugo and Frédéric (written to be played by the same actor, which was magnificently done both in Paris by Michel

Bouquet and in London by Paul Scofield) is a delightful decoration to the old stage device of indistinguishable twins. The many minor characters who add colour to the play – the wise old butler, the melancholy millionaire and his affected mistress, the booming dowager, the lunatic lepidopterist, the crazily sentimental companion – are all as heavily drawn as the characters of an animated cartoon but they make the play into a charade of flashing wit and fun. We scarcely notice the usual attack on the horrors of money, we sit back and hugely enjoy the parody of romantic verse à la Rostand in the ludicrous scene of the two old ladies rhyming about their youthful loves (not possible in the English version) – the whole play is kept on a hypnotising note of graceful and elegant mockery.

Yet once more he shows us purity in conflict with social corruption, once more it is a young girl who says *no* when compromise comes along. But how pathetically is that *no* expressed on this occasion, in the masterly scene described in Chapter I, where Messerschmann, fabulously rich, offers a large bribe to Isabelle, waves bundles of notes before her eyes, and is horrified when she refuses to take his money.

But the simple moral that money is a curse on the rich as much as on the poor is not to be taken too seriously, as it is here no more than a brilliant theatrical trick. As one famous critic wisely warned when *L'Invitation au Château* opened in English at the Globe, it is a play "to be shunned by the literal-minded". Let us beware of reading into this trip into glittering gaiety any more than was intended.

ARDELE

In one of his rare confidences to the Press, Anouilh said to an interviewer in 1946, just before leaving Paris to finish writing *L'Invitation au Château*, that when that was done he was going to stop writing for two years: "I shall abandon my characters, leave them to play by themselves, and look for another road along which to take my drama. . . ."

Certainly it was three years later that the next play was produced, and it marks a definite move into the realm of pathetic farce. The plays since this time have all been far more boldly contrived and have concentrated on bringing out of every situation as much pathetic absurdity as possible.

It would be shortsighted to toss these later plays aside because of their power to amuse – they are just as serious as ever; but the dramatic approach and patterns of thought are a little altered. Moreover he has chosen to publish the plays no longer under the old categories; henceforth they are labelled plain "farces" or "sparkling plays" (*Pièces Brillantes*). *L'Invitation au Château* was the first to be published under that designation.

It is impossible to read too much into *Ardèle* (1948), an ingenious mixture of drama and farce into which he has woven once again his bitter comments on life and love.* Going further than ever into his special field of "high farce" he lures us into a dubious kind of laughter that leaves a most poignant taste behind. In this angry, pessimistic work Anouilh shows himself a master at the height of his powers in every aspect of his craft: dialogue, situation and suspense, character and construction, all are magnificent.

In this play Anouilh sets out to show what the human condition (the flesh a slave to passion and the mind a slave to the corruptions of society) continually does to the pure sentiment of love. *Ardèle* puts love on trial, or rather shows the tests that face a pure love and before which it must in the end capitulate or die.

---

* *Episode de la Vie d'un Auteur*, a one-act trifle about the interruptions that keep a writer from his work, was presented as a curtain raiser with *Ardèle*, but had little success.

General Saint-Pé has summoned home his sister and his son to deal with a family crisis. His sister, the Countess Liliane, arrives with both her husband and her lover, between whom there is not a pin to choose.* All three look ludicrous as they appear in their Edwardian motoring attire: goggles and white coats, and the Countess in long green veils. The fantastic irruption on to the stage of this *ménage-à-trois* sets the tone for their farcical story, in which each is so busy watching the others that none can enjoy either sleep or love. They have motored straight over from the Casino at Trouville and arrive so early that the General is not yet down.

Nathalie, his daughter-in-law, receives them. She married Maxime, the eldest son (a notorious rake who had to leave for service in the Far East straight after the wedding night), and she has lived in the General's house ever since. It is not Maxime the General has sent for but Nicholas, the younger brother. This is the one Nathalie really loved, but they were too young to marry.

The rest of the General's household consists of himself and his mad wife, Amélie, who has gone crazed for love of him; Toto, his ten-year-old son;

* This point was ignored in the London production, where the actors who played the two parts could not have been more different. "Nothing should distinguish the Count from Villardieu," says Anouilh's stage direction. "The same moustache, the same high collar, the same monocle, the same bald spot on the back of the head, the same distinguished manners, and no doubt the same exclusive club. Perhaps the only difference between them: the size of the check in their motoring suits is not the same; but that is a *nuance*, no more."

the housemaid Ada, who is the lusty General's lifeline to the sensual world but who suffers his embraces with insolent indifference; and lastly Ardèle, a sister three years older than Liliane. This sister (whom we never see) is a hunchback well past forty, and she has fallen in love – to the utter disgust of the General and Liliane, for she is in love with a hunchback whom the General engaged as Toto's tutor. The General has sacked him, of course, but the man took rooms in the village and then the General had to lock Ardèle in her room because she tried to join him. She countered by locking the door on the inside and refusing all food. That is how things have stood for three days now.

The scene throughout the play is in the lounge-hall of the villa, with stairs leading up, first to Ardèle's room, and beyond to the General's room (from which we hear his wife's voice calling him every quarter of an hour with a shrill "Léon!", nearly identical with the cry of a peacock they keep in the garden). When Liliane and afterwards the Count and Nicholas speak to Ardèle, they stand outside her bedroom door, above the lounge. One side of the conversation is heard by all, but Ardèle's replies can only be guessed at. However public, therefore, these speeches are, they are in the nature of intimate appeals to Ardèle, trying to reach the heart of the matter without offending her sensibilities or exposing their own. In this delicate operation, full of irony for an expert like Anouilh, they all fail, only provoking protests from the family below and starting them off bickering about their own affairs, opening old sores, making them grope for solutions to the problems they have all avoided facing before. We get glimpses of the real feelings of these sophisticated, fantasticated people. They are caricatures with hearts, typical of Anouilh's special brand of satire which grafts universal pity on to minutely precise ridicule.

Ardèle is in the strongest possible position dramatically without ever appearing. She and the problems she has stirred up are never absent from the others' minds. She is a symbol but she seems no mere symbol when we are watching the play, so vivid is her presence in the locked room. No matter what is going on, whether the stage is empty or full, we feel her there. We guess at what she must be thinking of the despicable antics the rest of her family call by the name of love; we see them all freshly through her innocent eyes, for she suggests the criterion we judge them by.

Towards the end of this series of ludicrous appeals to Ardèle the General tells the Count (who is taking his turn at Ardèle's door and has used it to talk rather freely about the love-life of the others) to keep to the subject:

GENERAL: I have the feeling we're getting away from the point. Now, get back to Ardèle, or let me break the door down!

COUNT: Ardèle! We've never left Ardèle, General. Ardèle is love itself. If we persuade Ardèle to abandon the idea of giving her all to the hunchback, then there's hope for all of us; we can all be cured some way or other. . . .

Hullo? I'm sorry, Aunt Ardèle, we were cut off. What's that? You only live once, you say? Not quite so loud, please, I can't hear you very well. You have waited, you say, forty years and more for this joy which lifts you out of yourself? Go ahead, Aunt Ardèle, come out of yourself, throw your bonnet over the windmill, snap your fingers at the world, since either way you will one day have to go back alone into your hump to die. May I correct you, however, on one small point. Thank God one only lives once. It is amply sufficient. . . .

This is a brilliantly written act, in Anouilh's most movingly ironic vein, where he makes the fullest possible use of the fact that his principal character is behind a locked door.

In the last act it is the middle of the night and the stage is in darkness. We witness furtive comings and goings; when all is quiet, Nathalie and Nicholas meet secretly in the alcove under the stairs. She tells him how it came about that she did not wait for him, whom she loved, but married the brother who filled her with abhorrence. The choice she was faced with was losing her youth nursing a cross-

Lipnitzki

Lipnitzki

La Répétition at the Marigny. *Left:* Simone Valère and Jean Servais as Lucile and Héro. *Right:* Madeleine Renaud and Jean-Louis Barrault as the Countess and the Count ("Tigre"). They are dressed for a rehearsal of *La Double Inconstance* by Marivaux. Sets and costumes by Jean-Denis Malclès.

Colombe at the New Theatre. The final scene carries us back to the first meeting of Colombe and Julien (Joyce Redman and Michael Gough).

Colombe's dressing-room. Lagarde (Laurence Naismith) intrudes upon Julien and Colombe.

grained old aunt on whom she was a financial burden, or marrying immediately; as Nicholas himself was far too young she had accepted Maxime – that way she could at least be near Nicholas.

Through the window in the alcove they see a man creeping up to the house, making signals to someone. The man lets himself in, makes his way up to Ardèle's room, and is admitted. It is the hunchback.

Nicholas puts his arms round Nathalie, but she struggles not to be kissed. At last she confesses how she came to be truly unfaithful to him, by giving herself to Maxime and forgetting Nicholas in his embrace. She did not love Maxime but she returned his passion, abandoned herself to him.

NATHALIE: . . . The next morning I wanted to kill myself from sheer disgust. . . . But I didn't kill myself, and I waited humbly for the night to come again. And I've been waiting ever since. . . .

Now suddenly Amélie comes rushing from her bedroom, screaming. The whole household is roused. She points at Ardèle's room as she cries:

" . . . Stop them, I say! Stop them both! I am not mad! I know there's no stopping the beasts of the earth. But you, at least, stop calling to each other like cats all round me! Those two next-door! Stop them before I scream."

She is so insanely sensitive to her husband's secret lusting after women that she has grown to be conscious of the coupling of all creatures. Her tirade spends itself and she is just being helped back to bed when two shots ring out from Ardèle's room.

At this moment, the climax of the drama, the three men touch the peak of farce. The Count, Villardieu, and the General hurl themselves against Ardèle's door to break it down. They only manage to get in each other's way and are totally ineffective. It is practically a music-hall turn. At last Villardieu moves them away, takes a running leap, and throws himself against the door. It gives way, he falls flat on his face across the threshold, and the General grandly steps over him to take command of the situation.

When all have dispersed after the tragedy it is the children, Toto and his cousin Marie-Christine, who take the stage. They creep downstairs, dressed up in their parents' clothes, playing at "mummies and daddies". They start with silly love-talk, then quarrel and roll fiercely on the floor, biting and scratching each other.

TOTO (*rolling his "r's" to make it really passionate*): My dearest!

MARIE-CHRISTINE: My beloved one.

TOTO: My darling wife, I adore you!

MARIE-CHRISTINE: I adore you too, my dear little darling husband!

TOTO : Not as much as I adore you, my dearest love !

MARIE-CHRISTINE : Yes, I do, my dearest love, a hundred times more !

TOTO : No. No, you don't.

MARIE-CHRISTINE : Oh yes, I do ! I do !

TOTO : You don't ! You don't ! Because if you loved me less one day I'd kill you !

MARIE-CHRISTINE : No, my dearest darling, I'd kill you first !

TOTO : No, you wouldn't ! I would !

MARIE-CHRISTINE : No, you wouldn't. I would !

(*They face each other, stamping their feet and shouting.*)

TOTO : I'd kill you first !

MARIE-CHRISTINE : No, I would !

TOTO (*seizing and shaking her*) : No, I would, you silly little fool. I tell you it's me that loves you most !

MARIE-CHRISTINE : No, it isn't, it's me. It's me that loves you most ! (*She struggles to get free of him.*) You horrid beast ! You nasty pig ! You dirty black spider !

(*They fall to the ground, biting and scratching, shedding their finery, their hats flying. The curtain falls as Toto, yelling, rains blows on his cousin.*)

TOTO : I'll show you who loves you most, you little half-wit ! I tell you it's me who loves you most, you nasty pie-faced little horror, you beastly crawly caterpillar, etc, etc, etc.

This travesty is an appalling comment on all that has taken place, and brings the play to a conclusion.

The subject, then, is no more than a garish melo-drama – two hunchbacks fall in love, discover that their deformity makes their love ludicrous and inadmissible to society, and so kill themselves, every bit as if they were Romeo and Juliet once again. This extraordinary play might easily have failed to capture the audience's sympathy, but it is in fact saved, brilliantly, by the utter sincerity we cannot but feel throughout. The world it presents is a nightmare world of characters so soaked in their own isolated suffering that they are somehow all unbalanced – every character is trapped in his own temperament without hope of escape, victim of passions he can never explain. *Ardèle* is a terribly bitter play, but it holds the imagination as a piece of poetic theatre and rare artistic writing, and the characters, all in some way tortured by love, haunt the memory like the passion-ridden figures of Strindberg. The General, the Countess, Villardieu, the Count, Amélie, the invisible Ardèle, all are alternately farcical and pathetic until the ridiculousness of human loves and aspirations is painfully clear. "I realised the Countess, although having a serious part in the drama, must be played as farce," said Isabel Jeans in an interview during the London production, and it is this double-level writing and playing, so fantastic and yet so real, that provides the poignant pathos that illumines the play.

The period is once more in the imprecise *fin-de-*

siècle time that Anouilh uses to convey most effectively his sense of social decay. The play is in no way an attempt at tragedy, but the sheer poetic brilliance of the writing, and the flashing satire, would be enough to lift it above the mere expression of a savage mood. It has some of the wittiest and most theatrical moments I know in the whole of modern drama. The sharply etched characters, speaking in a racy and sparkling style, ride over the embarrassments of the subject in a series of mannered and carefully built speeches, while Anouilh's burning sincerity makes cynicism and contrivance equally acceptable.

Roméo et Jeannette ended on a note of attack on sexuality; in *Ardèle* lust is presented as a millstone round the neck of mankind, a revolting reality that must be faced, not wrapped in a conspiracy of silence. It is difficult to see how one can see or read this play without feeling its insistent sadness – for what passes for love in this world, to Anouilh is always doomed: it is palpably false and is no more than lust, or it is self-deception and leads inevitably to failure and loneliness. Both lust and love appear to be the great enemies of loneliness but in the end they are the most certain means of intensifying it. And the loneliness Anouilh conveys to us here has abandoned hope.

L'ECOLE DES PERES

Cécile or *L'École des Pères* (1949), play in one act, is a charming mannered trifle in almost pure Molière style. It is a very lightweight piece, its virtues being some quite brilliant dialogue and colourful characters.

The action takes place in a Louis XVI period garden. The testy but still young Monsieur Orlas is trying to persuade his daughter Cécile's companion, Araminthe, to accept his advances. He has "scratched at her door" before but been refused. Araminthe, an intelligent and sensitive girl, will have none of his over-confident wooing. A not very rich young man, Le Chevalier, is courting Cécile (and is in passing attentive to Araminthe as well), but Monsieur Orlas is strongly against the marriage. Indeed he is jealous of Le Chevalier and suspects his courting of Cécile to be a mere excuse for keeping near to Araminthe. Le Chevalier's father has just forbidden him to see them again, but he comes to ask Araminthe to help him elope that night with Cécile; on consideration Araminthe agrees, but we are given to understand that she has some further design. The lights go down to indicate night for the second scene and then begins a rapid comedy of mistaken identity. Monsieur Orlas prowls about in a huge cloak, come to prevent the elopement, as he suspects, of Araminthe; Cécile, heavily muffled, creeps out to her assignation – they speak in hoarse whispers and she takes him for Le Chevalier and he her for Araminthe. After some time Cécile recognises her father, but he doesn't recognise her until after he has properly declared himself, as he believes, to Araminthe. At this point, at the height of the confusion, Araminthe comes forward and explains her trick. Le Chevalier is brought out from the summer-house where he has been concealed, the two young lovers are united, Monsieur Orlas humbly proposes to Araminthe· she now accepts him and all ends well.

This amusing play is strongly divided in manner between the two parts – the first is excellent period character comedy written in very witty dialogue, and the second mere manipulation and plot. The play looks like a brilliant exercise in the two main types of Molière comedy – and the tendencies of the plays that follow confirm this impression.

LA REPETITION

La Répétition (or *L'Amour puni*), the "sparkling"
play that followed in 1950, is a modern pastoral
with a count and a governess in the place of prince
and shepherdess. But it is also the story of a pure
young girl whose freshness is brutally destroyed by
contact with middle-aged decay. The unusual structure of *La Répétition* is one of pure artifice – it is an
attempt to create a kind of double depth of plot and
character by building a modern drama superstruc-
ture over Marivaux's *La Double Inconstance*. The
characters, who belong to a wealthy circle in modern
decadent society, are rehearsing Marivaux's comedy
for a coming *fête*. Very soon it is manifest that the
leading players are in fact in almost exactly the same
relationship to each other as in the play. Anouilh's
idea was to make a mixture of dialogue from the
two levels and periods and mingle modern and
Régence decadence in such confusion that the audience
can hardly tell what world it is in.

The first two acts are of an astonishing brilliance
and the dialogue in them is a veritable *tour de force*.
While Anouilh's characters are rehearsing it is hard
to distinguish their own lines from the lines of
Marivaux's play. He has not copied a period style

but he matches it in taste and tone. In contrast to the concise manner of modern dialogue, in this "marivaudage" nothing is left out, everything is stated and extended with grace and distinction. There is delicate wit there, too. But when all is said much of the charm depends on this trick and to a modern ear, once the main artifice has been enjoyed, the play is long-winded.

The Paris production (with Madeleine Renaud and Jean-Louis Barrault) ran for a long season to packed houses, but the French do not mind long-windedness if the style is good. Nevertheless it was largely a *succès d'estime* for all concerned and will most probably not often be revived. I do not think it likely ever to have a London production, as the Marivaux pastiche makes its translation almost an impossibility.

The Count, called "Tigre", is a wealthy libertine who lives entirely for pleasure. He and his wife both have acknowledged lovers, for good taste makes them leave each other free in such matters. Into their household, appointed as governess to some orphans dependent on Tigre, comes a pure young girl, Lucile. Tigre falls in love with her and feels it is a love such as he has never known before. However, his highly intelligent wife is quick to see not only what is unsuitable socially in such an attachment, but also its difference in quality from all his previous *affaires*, for it threatens to change him completely. This will not do, so she brings out all her weapons: first the rather despicable trick of "losing" an emerald in the hope of besmirching Lucile's reputation and driving her away under a cloud; then she tries to have her seduced by Héro, Tigre's best friend. At the beginning the play is about Tigre and Lucile, but the second half falls to Héro and becomes *L'Amour puni* of the subtitle. Héro is a drunkard. Drink alone makes him able to face day after day of the empty life of pleasure that he and Tigre are vowed to. But Héro cannot live this pointless life with the enthusiasm that Tigre brings to it, because at nineteen he had a glimpse of something better: Evangéline. It was Tigre who persuaded him she would make an inadvisable match, and so it was broken off. Evangéline married someone else, was unhappy, and has since died. This old wound is reopened when Héro sees that Tigre has now found his Evangéline in Lucile. But he knows that Tigre will not, of course, be talked out of his prize as he himself was years ago ; Tigre will get what he wants, as he has done all his life.

From the moment the Countess asks Héro to seduce Lucile the play becomes the story of his revenge on Tigre, charged with all the bitterness that sprang from his own great disillusionment. The Countess gets Tigre out of the way by sending a false telegram. Héro comes into the room where Lucile is waiting up for Tigre to return home. He carries a bottle and two glasses and says that Tigre has just telephoned to say he cannot get back and would Héro keep Lucile company for a while. He cannot persuade her to drink with him and at first she does not respond when he tries to draw her out. But the more he does succeed in this the blacker grows his mood. She gives the perfect answers: she asks nothing of love; she wants love for its own sake and nothing more.

At last he can contain his bile no longer and breaks out angrily against his friend. Lucile asks him to leave her, but he stays, wallowing in self-pity now, and she listens to his story of the broken engagement with Evangéline. "That's what I'm here for," Héro then says: "Tigre owes me a girl in exchange." She is frightened but he reassures her; he only wants to talk to her, he says. After many torturing innuendoes he now tells her why Tigre is not back: he had come to a decision and asked Héro to explain to her that he thinks it best to break off their liaison before they are too involved. Héro tells this tale plausibly, not mincing his words at all, but he adds that Tigre told him to "try to console her". Lucile holds out for a few moments and then falls sobbing on the divan. Héro comes up to her.

With his trick he has destroyed her faith in love. Nothing matters any more. As he talks to her, his face bathed in tears, full of a drunken tenderness, she lets him caress her and take her in his arms.

Few seduction scenes I know have drawn such

poignancy from bitter motives. Héro, with the knowledge that comes from suffering, can play upon her every nerve and twist the knife cruelly to hurt her pride.

In the final act Tigre returns, but goes off again in chase of Lucile who has run away in despair. But she has many hours' start of him – he may never see her again. The play ends with Héro provoking the Countess's ridiculous lover to a duel, with the hope that thus he will end it all.

Anouilh's sudden change-over in the middle of the play is most disconcerting, for what begins as a delicate and brilliantly artificial comedy dives deep into a drama of the darkest hue. "It is *L'Invitation au Château* over again, but this time the card is edged with black," was Harold Hobson's comment after seeing the Paris opening. The unhappy character of Héro becomes, rather unwarrantably, the dark centre of the play and the issue of Lucile and the Count is far too rapidly disposed of.

La Répétition has an artificiality about it that makes it far less disturbing than usual – it is somehow too remote to be the direct attack on the audience, the prosecution of our basic values, that we have discovered in Anouilh hitherto.

COLOMBE

Colombe (1950) is also classed by Anouilh as a *Pièce Brillante*. This play shows us a tender romance crumbling to pieces before our eyes. The tone follows very much the pattern of the previous play – the first half amusing and witty, the dialogue leaping and racy, full of gaiety and comfortable laughter; then a sudden calm, and quickly the storm and a high dramatic tension.

Colombe takes up the love-story where the *Pièces Roses* used to put it down. The young lovers have married happily, and this is the "ever after."

The play opens in the wings of a theatre where Julien brings his young wife, Colombe, to see his mother, a celebrated tragic actress, Madame Alexandra. The young couple have been married two years and have a baby boy, but Colombe has never met Madame Alexandra since the first day she saw Julien. There is no love lost between him and his mother and he prefers living in poverty as a struggling composer to being in any way obliged to his mother, who he knows despises him. She has never approved of anything Julien has done, least of all of his marrying a girl from a florist's shop. Julien is leaving to do his military. service and wants to

entrust Colombe to someone's care; that is why
he has come, unwillingly enough, to the theatre.
Now that the moment is here he is apprehensive.
He feels his happiness is threatened, especially when
he sees Colombe, ignorant of the world of the
theatre, excited and intrigued by the novelty of
it all. . . . For he knows his wife is very pretty.

Julien, high-principled, uncompromising, ideal-
istic, morose and boorish in company, is the complete opposite of his brother Paul, who has always
been his mother's favourite. Paul acts as go-between
when their mother refuses to see Julien – he thus
helps to settle the matter of Colombe's future.
Madame Alexandra takes her under her wing (to
work in the theatre), so in theory Julien can leave
now without anxiety. Paul, though he has loud
taste in dress (we are at the end of the nineteenth
century again) and the looks of an idle libertine,
is charm itself. He has the gift of making a woman
feel that she is ravishing and exceptional. He flatters
her self-love by holding a mirror to her, for his
shining eyes reflect an image of her with all the beauty
she hopes she has. At his suggestion Colombe puts
on an exquisite dress and is introduced, as it were
by Paul, to a Colombe she never knew before.

Though she is not an austere idealist like Julien
she has been a sweet and patient wife to him, trying
hard to share his world. But he loves love for its
all-sufficient sake and she has to efface herself in
the shadow cast by its pure flame and do without

the little attentions and luxuries that would bring
her into the picture. Here in the theatre she has a
glimpse of how her beauty could kindle a flame to
illumine not love in the abstract but herself in the
light of love.

However, it is not at once that she understands
all this. In the meantime she keeps us wondering
just how artless her behaviour is. There are some
delicious scenes in which her naïveté, far better than
any defence based on virtue could have done,
utterly floors the poet (Robinet), the actor (Lagarde), and the manager (Desfournettes) who in
succession make advances to her. These three, like
Madame Alexandra and all those connected with
the theatre, are extravagant caricatures. It adds to
the beauty of Colombe to surround her with these
grotesque creatures – she is like a little girl among
a set of ugly dolls. Each of the three in turn invites
her to his home . . . "A drop of port, nibble a
biscuit – and we'll sign your contract. . . ." But
she plays them off one against the other. Only
Paul so far has really taken her home, and that time
they went through the piece she is preparing for
her admission to the Conservatoire, and he did not
offer her any port. . . . But at the theatre she
suggests he hear her through her lines again, as
there will not be another opportunity. They re-
hearse – a love scene, which she plays with seemingly artless sincerity. This time Paul has no
resistance left and his platonic façade crumbles.

Now Julien comes back on leave when he is not expected. He has had a letter about Colombe and he is already burning with jealousy. But Colombe welcomes him joyfully; it is just before the evening performance and she is in her dressing-room. The décor includes the corridor where the rest gather cynically to listen. She flings her arms round his neck, and they joke and laugh happily together. But it is not long before the ridiculous behaviour of Colombe's admirers brings Julien to the inevitable question. She denies everything and at one point it seems as if there is nothing more for him to say. But she babbles on too eagerly in her rôle of innocent but vivacious little wife making fun of all the fools who try to squeeze her hand, and she tumbles headlong into a real blunder. He calls her a slut and rushes madly out, leaving her in a faint. But Madame Alexandra takes command of the situation and orders everyone on stage. Colombe makes a miraculous recovery; in a few minutes Julien is back alone in the dressing-room. The more certain he grows that she never could have taken Lagarde or Robinet for a lover, the more convinced he is that she has taken someone.

While he is casting round savagely for the answer to this puzzle in walks Paul, carrying a bunch of flowers. For Julien it is like a revelation. He looks at his brother and suddenly says in a toneless voice: "So it's you." Paul's bantering evasions soon falter and they face each other in silence. Julien

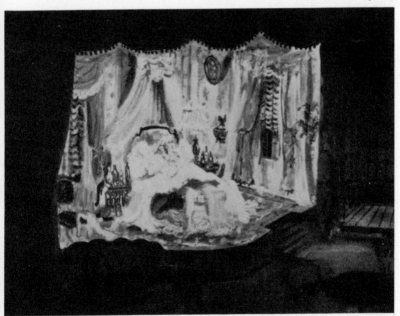

Sketches by Jean-Denis Malclès for the sets of *La Valse des Toréadors* at the Comédie des Champs-Elysées. *Above:* the drawing-room with door (*centre*) to bedroom. *Below:* the bedroom.

Lipnitzki

Lipnitzki

The General (Claude Sainval) n *La Valse des Toréadors* with (*left*) his wife, Amélie (Marie Ventura), and (*right*) Ghislaine de

murmurs: "Why? And why you?" Paul hedges no more; he is humble and abases himself. "What are you going to do?" he asks at last, but Julien does not move. He just cannot understand. This one great "Why?" is throbbing in his head too loud for him ever to hear an answer. Paul begs him to hit him, and when Julien, standing there with his fists clenched, shouts "No!", Paul bursts out against Colombe, calling her a dirty little whore and putting the blame on her. When he has finished Julien mutters:

JULIEN: Look at me!
PAUL: I can't.
JULIEN: Look at me!
PAUL: Hit me if you like. But don't ask me to look at you.
JULIEN (*lifting his head roughly*): Yes – you will look at me!

He stares into his face, examines Paul in detail, and finally even forces him to kiss him on the mouth – but nothing answers the great "Why?"

In the last act Julien tackles Colombe herself. The intriguing quality in the character of Colombe lies in the fact that we are never quite sure when she is acting, when the feeling she shows is pretended and when it is her own. This is what puzzled and captivated Paul when he first gave way to her appeal. The same question is now the burning problem with Julien: when did her acting begin?

It is torture to think that her love for him may never have been real, that all he has lived for was without foundation. This is the point on which the whole play revolves, and that is why the last scene – a dreamlike evocation of their first meeting, on the empty stage, when they fell in love – is an overwhelming climax, not just an appended flashback. Dramatically it brings bewilderment to the highest pitch of intensity and underlines all the conflicting truths about Colombe which Julien will never understand.

Which was the real Colombe ? And if the second is real, was the first not so ? The new Colombe at least has no time for the innocent little thing of two years before. She tells Julien that his sweet little Colombe only ever existed in his imagination. He seizes her and shakes her. "No!" he shouts. "You were just as I thought you! That *was* Colombe. You are . . . someone else. . . ." When he releases her she goes at once.

Thereupon Julien sinks into a mood of despair and thinks back to their first idyllic meeting two years before when Colombe brought Madame Alexandra's flowers to the theatre for her. That scene is now re-enacted, charged with pathos by the knowledge we already have of how completely this perfect love can go awry. Anouilh ends this scene, and the play, on Colombe's vehement assurances of undying love for Julien; she swears she will love him for ever, repeating confidently "Always!"

four times, bringing this romantic moment into poignant derision as the curtain falls.

There are two distinct and in fact conflicting tones in the play – the moving love-story as the central core and the furious caricature of theatre people and the back-stage idea of reality. In the London production the darker aspects of the play were toned down in the interests of the extravagant comedy; in Paris the whole play was more bitter.

In fact Anouilh appears in *Colombe* to show a need to laugh mercilessly at the things he had found so important hitherto, although it is clear that they are no less important to him, only viewed in a different way. In particular he presents his main character Julien unsympathetically, and leaves him to suffer by himself, pushing him aside, showing him for the nuisance he is to the rest of the world. In Julien's finest scene in the middle of the play, when he taxes Colombe with her infidelity, the dramatic scales are heavily weighted on her side, for Anouilh shows more understanding for impurity than ever before. And the purity of soul that made his earlier heroes and heroines so noble has here in Julien turned into unreasonableness. We cannot sympathise with his ideas, all we can do is recognise the sincerity of his feelings, dumped as he is in a world he will never understand. Hence some very cynical moments in this play – the kiss scene with Paul, for instance – that are dramatically very risky. The cynicism would be acceptable in itself, but the mockery is close to being distasteful, so the more deeply Anouilh succeeds in moving his audience the greater risk he runs of revolting them.

Yet in spite of intensely bitter moments we feel a mellowing in the author that softens the grievous resentment he has shown towards life up to now. Pity for the loneliness of men and understanding of their inhumanity to each other temper the usual ferocity of his revolt. We feel that the bitterest of Anouilh's romantic comedies has long been written, and that those to follow can never be so unrelievedly savage again.

LA VALSE DES TOREADORS

The last Anouilh play at the moment of writing goes further into the history of the General whom we first met in *Ardèle*. It is a play of arresting frankness, with the burning sincerity and searching wit of Anouilh's best vein of bitter farce. But *La Valse des Toréadors* has split the theatre-going public of Paris from top to toe – those who do not think it a masterpiece consider the play scandalous. However, even his most virulent critics admit that there are magnificently theatrical moments. The whole play is written in a mocking tone of high farce with some strikingly poetic passages in many of the General's longer speeches.

La Valse des Toréadors is what Anouilh was bound to come to one day – the pathetic story of a love that was a failure but that prolonged itself falsely and hypocritically, emptily and pointlessly, for a lifetime. The lovers are the General and his wife Amélie, who, you remember, is confined to her room, paralysed in both legs, half-crazed from jealousy and worry about the General.

General Saint-Pé, tortured by Amélie's continual calls and jealous accusations, is trying to dictate his History of the Moroccan War to his young secretary Gaston. The wife's calls interrupt them, so do the General's two silly grown-up daughters. When Doctor Bonfant arrives to see Amélie the General explodes and tells him how he and his wife have come to hate each other.

While the Doctor is examining Amélie in her bedroom Ghislaine de Sainte-Euverte suddenly and melodramatically appears. She is in love with the General, who is shocked to see her in his house, but she has come to tell him they are free at last, for they need no longer respect Amélie. She produces a passionate letter written by Amélie to the Doctor, which is proof of Amélie's infidelity.

Act 2 sees the General storming about, threatening a duel with the Doctor, who takes the whole thing very calmly, for there has never been anything between Amélie and himself. Ghislaine wants to leave with the General at once but he will insist on investigating and pushes her into another room while he talks it all out with the Doctor.

It seems that the General has been in love with Ghislaine for seventeen years – she was a young girl when he met her and waltzed with her at the Saumur Cavalry School Ball. She returns his love and has waited seventeen years faithfully for him. It has been the great love of his life, but he has never allowed himself to leave Amélie – out of respect for her deranged feelings he and Ghislaine have been only platonic lovers and have been content with romantic hopes.

GENERAL : . . . on the battlefield it's always simple enough, all you need do is refuse to contemplate death. In real life it's different. (*Pause. Then he adds dully*) : I don't like hurting people.

DOCTOR (*gently*) : Then you're sure to hurt people a lot, my dear fellow. And hurt yourself as well.

The General was always too timid to leave his tyrannous wife for an imagined paradise with Ghislaine, with whom he danced that unforgettable waltz at Saumur. He tells the Doctor how wretched he is, feeling that he has wasted away his life in loneliness, paying lip-service, by staying with

Amélie, to a love in which he long ago lost faith. He decides to face Amélie immediately and tell her of his resolution to leave her. But he comes rushing back from her room distracted – Amélie has gone, leaving a note clearly indicating that she is about to commit suicide. Doctor and General rush out in different directions to find her and stop her. Ghislaine hears all from the adjoining room and, thinking the General must love Amélie after all, decides to kill herself. She writes him a farewell note and draws out a dainty revolver which she aims at her temple – there is a click, it misfires. She steels herself and tries three times, but the revolver will not fire. She thinks for a moment and runs into Amélie's bedroom to throw herself through the window. There is a shout and after a moment the secretary Gaston enters carrying her – she has landed on top of him as he lay in the hammock in the garden. Gaston puts her down on the sofa, but in a daze she clings to him and calls him Léon (the General's name), tells him she loves him, makes him kiss her – he does so, thinking he must humour someone so evidently delirious. As he kisses her the General walks in carrying Amélie, whom he has found lying across the railway track. The General is furious; both women call him by name in their state of semi-delirium – he takes Ghislaine forthwith from Gaston, hands the boy his wife in exchange, and they carry them both away into other rooms to recover.

In Act 3 the General expands and tells the Doctor his conception of life and the contemptuous view he has of himself. He explains his futility and his sense of helplessness before the problem of relationship with other human beings :

GENERAL : I slap my chest like a gorilla and everybody says : ''There's a real man for you!'' Well, it's no more than an empty shell. There's nothing inside it. I'm all alone . . . and I'm afraid.

DOCTOR : Afraid of what ?

GENERAL : I don't know. My own loneliness perhaps. I'm a deserted child, who's now grown up. In Morocco, slashing with my sword at the Arabs – and God knows the pleasure I took in that ! – at Longchamp Tattoo when the President of the Republic presented me with the Grand Ribbon, at the brothel when I drowned everybody in champagne, I always felt like shouting for help. . . . I know what you will say. I should get inside myself ? I've tried that. I've got inside myself several times. Only, you see, when I did get inside there was never anybody there. So I soon grew frightened and came out to make a fuss somewhere outside and gain confidence in myself once again.

He confesses his weakness for women and says it is his horror of life that sends him running after them. Then he describes how different he feels with Ghislaine – his soul and conscience gnaw at him continually, except for the magic moments he spends with her :

"... It was an extraordinary thing that happened to me at that Ball at Saumur : I had invited a young lady very like all the others to dance – the colour of her dress or her hair must have attracted me – and then suddenly I realised I didn't feel afraid any longer. That was a marvellous moment, Doctor. . . . I introduced myself, asked her to dance, put my arm round her waist – and suddenly thought : 'This is wonderful ! What is happening to me ?' It was my soul leaving me in peace for the first time in my life !"

He bursts out into furious regret that he has not had the courage to go for his own wants and has been hamstrung by pointless scruples all his life. Then the Doctor leaves and the General begins dictating again to Gaston. After a few moments of farcical interruption from his two ludicrous daughters (who scream and fight for love of Gaston) he begins to tell Gaston, in a brilliantly comic scene, just what experience has taught him.

GENERAL : Life is one long family luncheon – boring, like every meal with the family, but necessary. First, because you have to keep yourself well fed ; second, because, if you don't want to sink to the level of the beasts of the field, it has to be done according to a long-tried ceremonial, with marked serviette rings, musical table-mats, different cutlery for every course, and a push-bell by your foot under the table. But, be warned! those are only the externals! It's a game you've decided to play because long experience has taught numbers of people – who were no less intelligent than you or I – that that was the only way out. So you have to play according to the rules: answer the children's questions, cut the pie into equal parts, scold the baby when he slobbers, fold your serviette properly and replace it in the ring – right up until coffee is served. But once the coffee is drunk – up, skip and away – the law of the jungle comes into its own again. You mustn't act like a fool, even then. . . . Of course, I can see what you'll say: "All that stuff isn't Machiavelli, it's middle-class hypocrisy. And what about ideals? What happens to the ideal?"

GASTON: That's right, General.

GENERAL: Well, my boy . . . the ideal looks after itself pretty well, thank you. I only wish we all kept as healthy by half! The ideal, my boy, is the lifebuoy. You're all in the water, splashing about, doing what you can not to drown – you can try to swim in the right direction, in spite of all the currents going the other way; the main thing is to use the classic breast-stroke based on the recognised principles – and if you're not a brute, never let the lifebuoy out of your sight.

You need do nothing else at all. Now, if you relieve yourself in the water from time to time, that's your business. The sea's big enough, and if the upper part of your body still looks as if you're doing the breast-stroke, nobody will have a word to say to you about it.

GASTON: But don't you ever reach the lifebuoy, General?

GENERAL: Never. But if you've any heart in you you never lose sight of it either. That's an achievement in itself. The odd few eccentrics who try any faster styles of swimming to reach it whatever the cost, only splash everybody else and drag along with them I don't know how many poor wretches who might have gone on quite happily paddling about by themselves – in the soup. Do you understand?

GASTON: General . . . do you think I could say something?

GENERAL: Of course, my boy. It's your turn now.

GASTON: I'm only twenty, General. I think I'd rather have a go at swimming fast, and be drowned.

GENERAL (*gently, after a silence*): You're quite right, my boy. It's shameful to grow old and understand. . . . Try nevertheless not to make other people drown as well, even for the best of motives. That's what's so hard – hurting other people, always, whatever you do yourself. I've got used to everything else, but not to that.

The General decides to go in to speak to his wife for the last time, and we are given their interview in entirety in Act 4. This is the most violent and the most controversial scene Anouilh has ever written, where the General's wife reveals her contempt and hatred of her husband and explains the exact character of what feeling she still has for him. It is merely a love of property, she loves him for the power she has over him, and in the last analysis for the suffering she can cause him. She taunts him with his cowardice and the impossibility of getting away from her, even in the grave. Then she insists on miming the dance at the Saumur Cavalry Ball – the same Toreador Waltz that has been the General's dream for seventeen years – that she remembers he was dancing when she went out to her carriage and home with a new-found lover. The General is horrified, but she forces him to dance a few tottering steps of nightmare mockery as she cries:

"Come and dance with your old skeleton, your old chronic disease, come on! Come and dance with your remorse! Come and dance with your love!"

Then she pins him in a corner and he suddenly puts his hands out to her throat and begins to strangle her as the curtain comes down.

Act 5 sees the General reassured by the Doctor that his wife only had a shock, and is more in love than ever. The General is mortified, and rails against writers of all kinds who tell stories of love and happiness in their books; the Doctor agrees with him that they are probably all pure inventions. Ghislaine returns from a walk with Gaston to tell the General she is in love with the boy and has consented to marry him. The General fumes and demands a duel, but at last, seeing the boy is a minor, sends for his guardian, the priest, to forbid the marriage. The priest has been waiting to tell the General some news: it appears that Gaston, who was a foundling, is the son of a lady named Léa who was seduced by the General himself in a garrison town twenty years ago. Léa has just confessed on her deathbed. They all press the General to permit the marriage now he knows that Gaston is his son, and the priest takes the others off to church to offer up a prayer to Providence. As the General sits alone in his room in despair, his wife calls again from her bedroom to make sure he is there as usual. He answers dully and sinks into gloom once more. A shadow appears by the French windows of the room, it is the new housemaid. Her entrance makes the General start; then he looks at her, sees how pretty she is, and remembers. He asks her name, and then:

GENERAL: What's all that fairy-story about having a soul? Do you believe in that? The Doctor's a fool. Put your broom down, my child. It's too late to begin sweeping now, and there's never enough dust on things anyway. Leave it. . . . Come, I'll take you round the garden and if you're a good girl I'll give you a rose. . . . (*He asks her timidly*): Will it bother you if I put my arm round your waist, Pamela?

PAMELA (*smirks*): No, sir. . . . But what will Madame say?

GENERAL: Madame will say nothing unless you tell her. Ah! that's it. . . . It's much better like this. Not that it has very much meaning, it's just that this way you feel less lonely in the darkness of this world.

(*They disappear through the window, a ludicrous couple, into the blackness of the night.*)

La Valse des Toréadors ends then on a mellow note of resignation, which is in fact, a note of dark defeat. In all the other plays there was also some strong measure of purity to relieve the blackness of Anouilh's world. But there is no powerful purity about *La Valse des Toréadors*, only the imbecility of Ghislaine and Gaston. The General is on the stage almost throughout, a tremendous rôle; for the structure of the play is exactly like a Molière character comedy where all depends on him. He is like Monsieur Jourdain, the Bourgeois Gentilhomme, or Argan in *Le Malade Imaginaire*, sublime in his weakness and self-delusion. He is continually amusing, but there is a heart-breaking quality in the picture of this extraordinary man who has hesitated before his impulses and bowed to the best of scruples for a lifetime, condemned himself to misery and mediocrity only to find he has suffered and sacrificed in vain – for it was not his wife he needed to get away from all the time, it was himself. We know the General is in a trap made of his own personality, imposed on him by the powers that be, and that he will always suffer in its grip. The conclusion Jean Anouilh draws from this play is put in the Doctor's mouth during the *deus ex machina* ending that reminds us of Molière's off-hand solutions:

"Poor fellow . . . would you like me to tell you the moral of this story? A man should never understand his enemy – nor his wife. . . . A man should never understand anybody else at all, in fact, or he dies of it. . . ."

3

Conclusions

WE have travelled a long way since *L'Hermine* and *La Sauvage*. Where are the intransigent young lovers now? Relegated to the peremptory match-making of the sub-plot – no more than grotesque reflections in reality of the dreams still struggling in an old man's memories. But Anouilh has not been unfaithful to those memories. The aspiring Lieutenant Saint-Pé is the one he loves best; if he loves the General too it is because a young man's heart still beats beneath the veteran's medals:

> "I've grown old almost without noticing it. My stomach got fatter and my hair got thinner, and more and more gold braid kept creeping round my sleeve as the years went by. And beneath the fancy-dress – a young man's heart still waiting to give his all."

Anouilh has at first sight a limited range of characters: a ridiculous mother, a resigned and degenerate father, a romantic young man, a rebellious young girl at fierce grips with reality, a treacherous friend. But on closer inspection they are all engagingly different: no one could mistake Thérèse's mother in *La Sauvage* for Georges' in *Le Rendez-vous de Senlis*; and no two gestures of defiance could be more basically different than the suicide of Jeannette and the voluntary death of Antigone. These stock framework characters of Anouilh's own brand of pantomime are all present still, but he has lost interest in the antics of Harlequin and Columbine and Pierrot, for does not Pantaloon contain them all? He is the fittest object for both laughter and pity.

We have already remarked a shifting emphasis in *Roméo et Jeannette*, where the cynical Lucien, as tart as the gooseberry he plays, steals the stage. Anouilh patently makes much less effort to secure our sympathy with his unlikely lovers – their great love-scene is wordy and disappointing, and their death reduced to a few lines of description by the feckless father. Lucien is bitter but he is still young; his disillusionment is fresh, his resentment unmellowed. With his lovers carelessly improbable and his cynic still sore from recent wounds, Anouilh wrote in *Roméo et Jeannette* his most anguished play.

The next serious play was *Ardèle*, where the character representing the pure ideal never appears at all, leaving the case to be thrashed out by an assortment of persons more or less broken by experience. To put Ardèle's defence in the hands of a man like the Count is indeed a transformation. This is not a play about pure love but about disillusioned people measuring themselves against the dreams of their youth.

La Répétition starts off on the lines of earlier plays, but turns in the end into a study of Héro's revenge – for which we cannot altogether withold our sympathy, for we see through him right into the heart of a corrupted man. He is the villain of the piece, but not for nothing is he called Héro.

Colombe, which followed, shows the idealist at his least lovable. And the girl who compromises her purity now seems to do less violence to her personality that way than when she tries to straighten and narrow herself to the faithful love of her husband.

Finally *La Valse des Toréadors* is wholly dedicated to the old General's case, and the change is now complete. He is idealist passion mellowed by despair – the bright vigour of spring has long been dulled and autumn's resignation tinges him with all the sombre colours of regret. His is the season of ripe thoughts that have lost their bloom.

As all Anouilh's characters speak with extraordinary conviction we can only assume that no one of them speaks directly for the author more than another. Antigone the fatal idealist, Lucien the disillusioned one, Colombe who says yes to life, the General who would have liked to . . . it is as if their creator were standing beyond a stained-glass window: the figures depicted on the glass are not self-portraits (there may be a family likeness, as is common enough between a painter and the faces he creates), but his shadow behind them makes some become obscure and colourless while others stand out in all their radiance. As the sun moves into its decline those who speak for age and acceptance are better illumined than the pure angels trumpeting at the top; but Anouilh is no unmovable sundial for the sun to play upon – within the limits of the sun's course he is master of his own shadow.

Hidden in the disturbing violence that has distressed so many people and turned them away from Anouilh's work is the expression of a deep and unremitting poetic anguish. He has grown more tolerant, more ready with pity, though still basically resentful – for the source of his pity is still a passionate feeling of disgust at the wretchedness of human destiny. He seems to have grown to an ever more terrible understanding of the way in which petty defects and concessions, small meannesses and betrayals can turn life into a vile, festering sore. This genuine sense of pity and distress that is never lacking in Anouilh is a compensation for the harshness that his resentment against fate drives him to show. Some of the most moving moments of the plays are to be found where that profound pity comes to expression.

Everyone is guilty of those petty betrayals, and everyone knows he is. So the character in a play who commits one, and realises it, is assured of sympathy, for he represents common humanity however much he is made an object of laughter; he is always pathetic as well as grotesque.

Laughter and pity are combined in Anouilh's work to give a brand of uproarious and pathetic satire which is all too exact for the terrible times of individual helplessness we live in. I do not believe that he himself regards ours as a more helpless period from the point of view of the individual than any other period in the history of man, but perhaps it is because he has so strong a sense of man's ultimate defencelessness that he has become in drama the spokesman of an age acutely conscious of it.

In the 'twenties, when Anouilh was beginning to write, there was a mood of youthful intolerance. Everything old and traditional was thrown overboard; parents were left behind; youth took the helm. But in its own individualistic way it still followed many of the old rules of navigation. The disillusionment of the 'twenties was not so complete as it seemed. We can see now that the people who experienced it still had faith in reason and progress although they had lost their faith in God. They could not afford to pity those who made mistakes; now we cannot afford not to, for we all stand condemned.

The settings of Anouilh's plays carry us back through those times to an earlier period – a vague half-way house between the solid bourgeois confidence of the pre-Dreyfus decade and the uneasily

self-righteous idiocy that followed. An officer in
the trenches in the 1914–18 war might have dreamed
of waking to convalescence in one of these stately
homes of France among charming, carefree gentry
of a happy era before all the horror began. Florent
in *La Sauvage* would certainly have been a generous
host to wounded soldiers; so would Léocadia's
lover, and Madame Desmermortes in *L'Invitation au
Château*. This is the social background of the prosperous characters. It has the charm of a past epoch,
with the added piquancy of being recent enough to
be remembered and yet as unrecoverable as the
innocence of childhood.

The less prosperous Anouilh characters are either
second-rate artists (actors and musicians) or in some
vaguer, idler occupation which satisfies neither the
desire for security nor self-respect. They are root-
less people and lonely, but they are never frankly
tramps.

This general background to the plays has not
changed in two decades, but the mood has. The
'twenties have given way to the 'forties and 'fifties.
It is not youth that speaks any longer, though
Anouilh never repudiates the truths of youth. The
perspective is different and these truths are perhaps a little less important now compared with the
human beings who so poignantly attempt to keep
faith with them and fail. Anouilh is writing pure
comedies of character now like Molière; he is
perhaps in the process of adding a deeper meaning

to farce (what I have called once or twice here "high farce", for want of a term to describe this new dimension), as the genius of Molière gave meaning to comedy that it had never had before.

Why is it that we have such a strong sense of universalities and abstract values in Anouilh's plays ? We do not talk of his play about an actress's daughter who went off with a roving musician, but of the slut who found a pure love which could not make her clean; not of the governess of an orphanage whose employer makes her his mistress, but of the pure young girl who brings a new vision of life to a man who has cared only for pleasure. And so on for them all. We deal in abstractions when we recount his themes and see them in simplified but essential terms. We say : "Colombe is so feminine in her adaptability; there's a bit of an actress in every woman" – forgetting that Lucile and Thérèse, for instance, have nothing in common with Colombe. We constantly find ourselves generalising like this.

It is partly that the characters themselves are given to truisms. Take Orpheus :

"For in the long run to be two is unbearable. . . . Two prisoners . . . each tapping on the wall from the depth of his cell. Two prisoners who will never see one another. Oh! how lonely we are. . . . "

Or M. Henri from the same play:

> "My dear chap, there are two types of beings.
> The name of one is legion, he is prolific,
> cheerful, malleable clay; the man of this type
> munches his meals, begets his children, plies his
> trade, counts his pennies, year in year out,
> through epidemics and wars, on into ripe old age;
> he is of the people who merely exist, the everyday
> people, the kind you cannot imagine dead. Then
> there are the others, the noble, the heroic. The
> kind you can very well imagine stretched out,
> pale, with a bullet hole through their skulls; tri-
> umphant, with a guard of honour one minute,
> or marched off between two policemen, as the
> case may be: the cream. . . ."

Or the General from the latest play:

> " . . . There's a sensual pleasure in knowing
> you have a soul, too, Doctor. The materialists
> don't know anything at all about pleasure. . . .
> It's just wonderful stealing a moment of igno-
> miny now and then. A man never has many in
> this life, in any case, with all the scruples he's
> bothered with."

The plays are full of lines like this, and in all of
them we perceive a large spark of truth, enough
at least to sustain the argument, point the comedy,
or splash the speaker with their irony.

More than that, he gives us characters who are so

clear-minded about their essential intentions, their words are so much to the point, that they speak for all who are like them. His words, like poetry, transcend the immediate situation, extract the essence. La Surette in *Colombe* is an example among many. He is the mean and nasty old man who writes to Julien, informing on Colombe to excite his jealousy. He has failed in life himself and as secretary to Madame Alexandra is bullied all the time. He is the cuckold *par excellence* who has made a thorough, morbid study of his condition. He is a specialist who can pierce the whole process of cuckoldry and takes us to the heart of the matter. Here he sets out to show Julien that the cap fits him also – he will wear it in the end and perceive that he was bound to from the start.

JULIEN : I shall question her.

SURETTE : Do you think she'll tell you ?

JULIEN : If she won't, I shall question them.

SURETTE : All five ?

JULIEN : Yes.

SURETTE : And what about the sixth, the seventh, and the eighth ?

JULIEN : Who are they ?

SURETTE : The ones you'll begin to suspect after you've questioned the first five. . . . Oh, there's no end to it, now, my young friend. Once it's happened it can happen again ; and with anyone – literally anyone – that's the trouble. Never assume that the man who attracts your wife will necessarily seem agreeable to you. That's rule one. Oh, no! It may be just a voice on the tele-phone, a photograph in a drawer, a letter in a strange handwriting. . . . Who? Who? Who? You'll never stop asking yourself that question now. When she buys a hat – who's it for? When she sings in the bath – who's it for? The rouge on her cheeks, the scent behind her ears – who is it she takes all this trouble for? Not for you. Oh no – that's long past, the time when it was you she was after. It's all for some mysterious Monsieur X. Perhaps you know him, perhaps you don't. But from now on, my dear boy, he's going to be far and away the most important person in your life.

In the case of La Surette one word describes his condition or his "humour" as Ben Jonson would have put it. Most of Anouilh's characters need more than one word to describe them, but they still represent the essence of their predicament, all of its *nuances* explored and defined with uncanny precision in a style unequalled in modern dramatic writing.

But the factor that lies deepest in this universality is that Anouilh's characters present in conflict with each other forces which we all know within ourselves. When we are watching one of his plays, responding to it, small pieces of ourselves are picked from us and distributed among the characters;

they are at moments all so true that we feel
a sort of personal disintegration in progress that is
most unsettling. This is true of many playwrights
but Anouilh more than most knows how to people
his stage with the conflicting aspects of human
nature in the form of round, solid human beings,
not mere types and symbols. For however clearly
and boldly the characters are drawn, we have a
sense of their human frailty and complexity.

Every serious character in Anouilh sooner or
later is a victim of his own lack of faith – in love,
in life, or simply in himself. There is no question
anywhere of faith in God. Hopelessness and mistrust reign through the serious plays and all is reduced to a world of individual despair. The hero
does not believe in anything any more in the later
Anouilh – save his own guilt and loneliness. Situations from play to play are often parallel, characters
are often preoccupied with the same problems, but
they are themselves always distinct. The relationship between Georges and Robert in *Le Rendez-vous
de Senlis* resembles that of Tigre and Héro in *La Répétition*, but the characters are quite unlike. The
disillusionment of the Count and Countess in
Ardèle may have sprung from a situation like Julien
and Colombe's. Marc in *Jézabel* faces the same
choice as Thérèse in *La Sauvage*. But all these characters have their own very marked individual ways of
dealing with their problem.

His themes are in fact elementary, often naïve,

yet upon these simple foundations he constructs the most powerful and poetic plays. They all revolve round a pure love and show it contrasted with lust, or respectable contentment, or the possessive feelings that parents have for their children. But beyond this it is surprisingly hard to generalise about Anouilh and his drama. Yet his trademarks are unmistakable – poignant caricatures mixed into a story of romantic love told in quite unforgettable scenes of comedy or pathos, or both, that rank with the best in dramatic literature. As the years go by he is shifting his comedy across from the minor characters, spreading it, and making his gloomy principal characters more and more disarmingly comic.

On reflection it will be seen that his characters never will be integrated. The dilemma can never be solved honestly in Anouilh's terms. There is a basic conflict in human nature and it is on this that Anouilh builds all his drama, for he sees the whole of life divided over the issue for ever, without end. There are two truths – the truth of innocence and the truth of experience – which never can be reconciled. The first is pure, intransigent, beautiful, *rose*; the second is cynical, corrupt, repulsive, *noir*. You can resolve the conflict only by some sort of cheating, because it is by definition irresolvable. So Anouilh paints the whole of life in those terms – adolescent purism violently proclaiming the eternal human visions of absolute love and absolute justice, tearing itself to pieces in despair. It soon has so overwhelming a sense of isolation, so little faith in youth's power to stay whole, that it chooses death or some course symbolical of death rather than barter purity for life, that is revealed by experience as nothing but compromise and endless hypocrisy. The result in both old and young – a desperate feeling of loneliness – is the exact opposite of the most glorious of all youth's rosy dreams, the vision of perfect communion in love.

In other words, the dramatic conflict is not so much between one character and another as between the main character and the lessons of experience. Sometimes the other people are the symbols of experience: for example, Eurydice's manager, or Barbara for Georges in *Le Rendez-vous de Senlis*. It is therefore not by the development of character but by its manipulation that he works out the action and expounds what he considers to be the truth about humanity. This "playing" with his characters (infusing them almost with the author's sense of his aim) was what in one of his rare interviews with the Press he said he had discovered when writing *Le Voyageur Sans Bagages* in 1936:

"If a child wants to stay away from school he pretends he is ill, and his parents do not believe him. But if when he is playing with friends a week later he again pretends to be ill, he will probably succeed in making it extraordinarily

realistic, the expressions on his face will be quite
alarming . . . because this time he will really be
'playing'. . . .

"In 1936 I discovered that a subject did not
necessarily have to be treated in a rigid form, in
the natural simplicity or even crudity it has at
first. I realised that the dramatist could and
should *play with* his characters, with their passions
and their actions. *Le Voyageur Sans Bagages* was the
first of my works in which I 'played' in this way.
. . . To 'play' with a subject is to create a new
world of conventions and surround it with spells
and a magic all your own. . . ."

Anouilh is indeed at his best when working on his
characters, "playing" with them as he calls it –
not creating the fiction for some ulterior motive
but playing make-believe for its own sake.

That is how he excels in romantic or fantastic
comedy; he knows the value of improbability and
is never frightened of the critic's short-sighted com-
plaints that his plays are "contrived", for he
writes in a tone where contrivance makes for
strength rather than weakness. No one would
question the fact that *L'Avare* is contrived, but the
tone of the comedy imposes Molière's convention
of artistic truth. Anouilh has the same unerring
sense of poetic licence and pays very little attention
to the details of realism – that is one of the
measures of his dramatic gift. In *La Valse des*

Toréadors he ends on a perfect *deus ex machina* – a priest brought out of the pantry to reveal the secret of Gaston's parentage, unite this long-lost son with his father, and in two or three minutes tie up all the loose ends of the play.

But Anouilh adds a naturalness even to this kind of contrivance that touches us indirectly – for does not this very 'playing' show up the helplessness not only of his characters but of the human race itself. As we see in *Ardèle*, artificiality of relationships, and a mannered and highly theatrical presentation of character make it possible to countenance rather appalling ideas and find them diverting. His creatures are puppets of flesh and blood. In the plays he manipulates the strings, but if it were not him we feel it would be *"l'autre là-haut"* as Lucien refers to God in *Roméo et Jeanette*. The contrived ending has been steadily eschewed in modern dramatic writing, especially in England, and it is proof how hard-dying realism is in the theatre that the contrived ending is often considered by definition to be an admission of defeat. Perhaps Anouilh's most re-markable innovation is to apply this ''playing'' technique to drama as well as comedy, for to him (as to Molière, whose galley of portraits started in a set of *commedia dell'arte* figures very similarly to Anouilh's in many ways) the characters are far more real than the plot.

In technique Anouilh is an unashamed child of the theatre with no intellectualism and no literary pretensions to lure him from what he knows are the bones of drama. For his central characteristic is simplicity, direct communication in both language and idea. So much is this a primary concern that he has developed the most rigid set of conventions of any modern playwright – words and ideas, phrases and incidents, details of character are repeated deliberately. Anouilh asks us to recognise and accept the eternal conflict between innocence and experience: once we have agreed to see this in his terms – that is, accepted his convention – we can plumb the depths of emotion that his characters offer.

As for his magnificently theatrical style, Anouilh writes in the poetic tradition of this century's best French drama. He shares with many other playwrights the conception of drama as in essence poetic – stirring and reflective, arresting and impressive in language, dotted with longer speeches of beautifully chiselled prose that are poems in themselves, taking its inspiration in its characters but transcending them into a world of universal sympathy, not delving into them with clinical inquisitiveness. Anouilh's lyricism, his satire of the human rather than the social, his plea for purity and sincerity with no tinge of moralising, his indifference to allegations of contradictions in his works, are in this tradition of poetic truth.

Jean Giraudoux, Armand Salacrou, Henri-René Lenormand, Jean Sarment, Charles Vildrac, Jules

Romains, and many others have all struggled with the confusion of feeling that their experience of life has brought, and like Anouilh have expressed their doubts about common human values; they have all explored the uncertainty of spirit of modern man. Anouilh's total refusal to accept society's emotional values without scrutiny is the most complete of many. But no French dramatist before him has so persistently stressed the utter loneliness of man and the inescapable state of misunderstanding in which we must always live with our fellows.

In his romanticism Anouilh shows particularly close affinity to Jean Giraudoux, France's leading poetic dramatist between the two World Wars. But Giraudoux was eminently French in all he wrote; it is doubtful whether the entrancing phantasy of this superb French stylist can ever be fully rendered in English. His magical dialogue spelled disaster to dramatic realism at the beginning of the 'thirties; his young women in their devastatingly pure state of virtue brought a new radiance to innocence on the stage that put it in a world apart. Giraudoux's dictum *"Je connais les jeunes filles et leur intransigeance"* might be an Anouilh motto. In colourful language that is the instrument of the poetic vision – with Giraudoux "precious" because of his flight from the commonplace, with Anouilh stark and bitter because of his venom against the commonplace – these two, and indeed all these modern French poetic dramatists, have cut to the heart of their contemporaries' sense of loneliness. With their non-realist characters they emphasise man's outer involvement and his inner isolation – they give him a grotesque decorated envelope and slip a letter of lonely and poetic grief inside.

Before Sartre had made his specially atheistic brand of existentialism a household word Anouilh was basing dramas upon three of its main tenets, all typical of the mood of our time. There first the conviction that everyone is alone, that no full or adequate contact can be made with others and every attempt to do so leads to frustration, to erosion of the self. Secondly, one is no more than the sum of one's past actions as seen through the eyes of others. At every moment we are living up to a picture which others have made of us, containing all the falseness of the half-reported past and charged with a sense of guilt that vitiates our freedom of choice in the present. (What could more clearly illustrate this than *Le Voyageur Sans Bagages* – portrait of a man who has no past and is offered one which is the sum of all that his relations remember of him ?) Finally the existentialist believes that he is free to make his own values and need not accept anyone else's. This is precisely the theme of *La Sauvage*, where Thérèse acts according to her inner conviction of what is suitable for her; she has to make a decision to which she can be true, and so she makes one which is true to her life-style as she feels it, not as others think it; it is a despairing gesture of defiance, but it is the only ultimately true gesture she can make.

Gabriel Marcel recently defined the existential play as one "where the main characters are in fact called upon to decide exactly what they are". In the massacre of modern war, in air-raids, in prisons, and in concentration camps, the central issue has stood out clear for all to see: men, individuals, are what they *are* simply by virtue of the power of decision that is in them. But it is in the actual fact of decision that the importance lies for the existentialist. In Gabriel Marcel's own plays this decision or choice, and the assertion of self that it implies, is the focal point; in Sartrian drama the decision of the main character is almost made by the other characters immediately connected with him. Both these very competent dramatists are too tied to their theses to let themselves go – they will never "play" with their characters for fear of their getting out of hand. Anouilh's emphasis is on the whole pattern of experiences that go to make up the characters, on the weight of guilt and memory that he brings at the crucial point to the making of the decision. That is why his plots can be melodramatic but his characters remain poetic and memorable – how much more directly moved we are by them than by the superficially more realistic figures in the plays of Sartre and Marcel.

Anouilh has had no real contact with the existentialist movement and what he has in common with it stops there. But it is an extraordinary coincidence, and one that shows how close his feelings are to the mood of the time, that he should stress these very points well before they were formulated into a popular philosophy of pessimism expressing the general disorientation of this generation.

In any case he is a dramatist, not a philosopher; the ideas he manipulates are aimed at an emotional not an intellectual effect. It is as if the dramatist were painting a picture with a palette of vivid ideas but in fact the figures take up the whole of his attention. He is tempted to "play" with them and and try all the colours on his palette until each figure stands out boldly, separately, sufficient justification in itself. The ideas are mixed to an infinity of shades, and spread to the best advantage, but they remain only part of the materials with which the artist works. The things he says are in the end less important than the way he says them. It is the characters that make his ideas so fascinating. Without those delightful figures to present them, the ideas would be no more than right or wrong – were the ideas his main concern, Anouilh in fact, as Oscar Wilde put it, "would fall into the careless habits of accuracy". Nobody calls La Fontaine a bad poet because the *Fables* advise conduct of a quite amoral opportunism.

No, the characters and the poetry that is in them, the brilliantly sensitive manner in which he builds up our relationship to them and swings us into their tragic or fantastic predicament – those are the specially dramatic virtues of Jean Anouilh. All depends on the extraordinary personages on his stage. And how basically allied they all are beneath their striking differences. One remarkable thing first concerning his heroines : they are none of them really viewed as women by the heroes. They are girls rather than women, and so can be regarded as comrades. For the terms used by the heroes when speaking of their loved ones are astonishingly similar : "little fellow" Florent calls Thérèse in *La Sauvage* ; Orpheus says to Eurydice, "it is as if we were brothers" ; in *Roméo et Jeannette* Frédéric tells Jeannette, ". . . so you are going to be my wife tonight – wife and little brother all in one . . ." ; Lucien in the same play tells Frédéric, "You've lost in advance . . . because one night in a month's time, or a year, or ten years from now, when you think you're holding your little friend in your arms, you'll realise all of a sudden that you're no better off than the rest, and that it's only a woman, there's nothing more there after all. . . ." The ideal love is conceived in terms of a youthful camaraderie between the sexes – what Hubert Gignoux has aptly termed "a sort of mixed Boy Scouts".

His heroes and heroines are all more or less retarded idealists, from the misguided Frantz in the first genuine play to the impenitent General in the last. And all spiritual adolescents have a common emotional virginity that makes them equal in a way that other men and women are not. At that age, ignorance of sexual relationships tends to make one attribute the common qualities of friendship to one's first love affair. But the young idealist in love is already a little disillusioned with the best friend; that is why he has turned elsewhere, for the search for the perfect communion of love has led him to new hunting grounds. Early in youth he has a glimpse of the pure white creature he longs for and he pursues her vainly for the rest of his life with the hounds of despair at his heels. As the years pass he begins to see that the hounds will always be too swift for him.

Indeed Anouilh's attitude throughout his plays is that of an idealist of twenty, with more than the usual experience of life and marked from the beginning with the pessimism of maturity. The astonishing thing is not that he can keep on writing the same theme but that he can arrive at such a variety of solutions. The reason is that he has not a philosophy but an attitude; his view is purposely limited to seeing such things as a young idealist sees and ignoring aspects that would only occur to an older observer. Hence his heroes reject their parents but are not parents themselves*; they revile money

* The only exceptions to this are interesting: Colombe and Julien, whose infant child serves the purpose of pointing Julien's violent attacks on his own mother but is quite unimportant; and the General, who in *Ardèle* has failed to establish any contact with his sons, and who in *La Valse des Toréadors* is horrified at the sight of his two gawky daughters: "They have shared their mother's virtues out between them: enough to bring misery to two poor fools instead of one."

whether they have it or not; ambition, careers mean nothing to them, they cannot let work loom large in their lives, for they are occupied with freeing themselves from family trammels. They are given to exaggeration and sudden impulses, and their moods swing violently from gay to sad and back, always veering, like Anouilh's plays, to new conclusions. Being young the idealist hero is incomplete. But a person of twenty – or any age – is a valid human being as he stands, not for what he might be at fifty. And so is every Anouilh play. Each must stand or fall as a work of art, not as a chapter in a developing philosophy or a corner of a larger picture.

Jean Anouilh's plays so far, then, have the attitude of youth clothed in the observation of age. But the action of the plays is taken by the young, or depends on a late-developer (like Ardèle) or on an aged adolescent (the General). It is at twenty that life poses these vast problems and demands a decision. At twenty we are not aware of living in a glass house; we think we are in the open, so we are utterly careless about throwing stones.

As we grow older we temporise, we watch others, we take half measures and hope for the issue to be shelved, we trim our moral ambitions, tame our irritations. We accept Madame Tarde, and the Renauds, and Creon and the rest as too common a tale to be shocking. Anouilh's plays are in fact the product of an obsession with an idealist's problems, not of a reasoning out of them. They are a vivid presentation of a lifetime's mood.

But there is in them a freshness and verve, a dramatic vigour and agility of mind that are constantly carrying us beyond youth into the broadest fields of human emotions. Anouilh has himself after all said yes to life, and he must more and more explore the virtues and the happier meanings of that essential compromise. The youthful feelings are still vivid, and their impact even more far-reaching, but their expression is tempered by age and by an increasing mood of pity rather than anger. We can expect Anouilh to be perhaps less passionate in the future, but warmer, to treat the plot more and more as a plaything, but to go on adding to the stature of his characters, deepening both the pathos and the humour of their situation – becoming more and more the poet of their loneliness.

"My heart is not made of stone . . . ," says the General (formerly, and to a large extent still, Lieutenant Saint-Pé). "But I am economising on tears. I'm growing old."

TABLE OF ANOUILH PLAYS

Title	Production Dates Paris	London
HUMULUS LE MUET (1929)	—	—
MANDARINE (1929)	1931	—
ATTILA LE MAGNIFIQUE (1930) (Never published or produced)	—	—
L'HERMINE (1931)	1932	—
JÉZABEL (1932) (Withdrawn by Anouilh from London production)	—	—
LE BAL DES VOLEURS (1932)	1938	1951
LE SAUVAGE (1934)	1938	1957
LE PETIT BONHEUR (1935)	—	—
Y AVAIT UN PRISONNIER (1934)	1935	—
LE VOYAGEUR SANS BAGAGES (1936)	1937	1959
LE RENDEZ-VOUS DE SENLIS (1937)	1938	1957
LÉOCADIA (1939)	1939	1955
EURYDICE (1941)	1941	1950
ORESTE (Fragment, 1942?)	—	—
ANTIGONE (1942)	1944	1948
ROMÉO ET JEANNETTE (1945)	1946	1949
MÉDÉE (1946)	1954	1955
L'INVITATION AU CHÂTEAU (1947)	1947	1950
ARDÈLE (1948)	1949	1951
EPISODE DE LA VIE D'UN AUTEUR (1948)	1949	—

Table of Anouilh Plays

L'ECOLE DES PÈRES (1949)	1949	1957
LA RÉPÉTITION (1950)	1951	1961
COLOMBE (1950)	1951	1952
LA VALSE DES TORÉADORS (1951)	1952	1956
L'ALOUETTE (1952)	1953	1954
ORNIFLE (1954)	1955	—
PAUVRE BITOS (1956)	1956	1963
L'HURLUBERLU (1958)	1959	1966
BECKET (1959)	1959	1961
MADEMOISELLE MOLIÈRE (1960)	1960	—
LA FOIRE D'EMPOIGNE (1960)	1960	—
L'ORCHESTRE (1962)	1963	(Bristol, 1967)
LA GROTTE (1963)	1963	1965
MONSIEUR BARNETT (1967)	—	(Bristol, 1967)
LA BELLE VIE (1967)	—	—

The dates in parentheses indicate the years in which the plays were written by Jean Anouilh.

Le Bal des Voleurs and Ardèle were both produced out of town before a London production was risked. Le Rendez-vous de Senlis was played in French by André Barsacq's Company at the Edinburgh Festival of 1951.

GAYLORD

PRINTED IN U.S.A.